DEEP JUSTICE JOURNEYS:

50 ACTIVITIES TO MOVE FROM MISSION TRIPS TO MISSIONAL LIVING

KARA E. POWELL AND BRAD M. GRIFFIN
FROM THE FULLER YOUTH INSTITUTE

WITH CONTRIBUTIONS BY

TODD BRATULICH • RANA CHOI PARK • APRIL L. DIAZ
TERRY LINHART • DAVE LIVERMORE • KURT RIETEMA

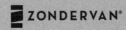

ZONDERVAN.com/
AUTHORTRACKER
follow your favorite authors

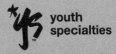

youth
specialties

youth specialties

Deep Justice Journeys Leader's Guide: 50 Activities to Move from Mission Trips to Missional Living
Copyright 2009 by Kara E. Powell

Youth Specialties resources, 300 S. Pierce St., El Cajon, CA 92020 are published by Zondervan, 5300 Patterson Ave. SE, Grand Rapids, MI 49530.

ISBN 978-0-310-28603-5

Cover design by SharpSeven Design
Interior design by Mark Novelli, IMAGO-MEDIA

Printed in the United States of America

09 10 11 12 13 14 • 20 19 18 17 16 15 14 13 12 11 10 9 8 7 6 5 4 3 2 1

CONTENTS

INITIAL STEPS: GETTING THE MOST OUT OF YOUR JOURNEY

BY KARA POWELL AND BRAD GRIFFIN

Your summer mission trip to Mexico is four months away.

Your Saturday breakfast for families who are homeless is four weeks away.

Your talk on the importance of service is four days away.

This book is for you.

If you're like most youth workers, you want your students to get a taste of service that leaves them hungering for more. Because you know service changes people, your ministry calendar offers a buffet of opportunities—a short-term mission trip here and a half-day convalescent home visit there. But if you're honest with yourself, you sometimes wonder if your students are feasting on all God offers or merely scraping up the crumbs.

You're not alone.

Recent research suggests service trips and experiences might not be producing the spiritual and relational "bang" we expect—at least not in the long term. Consider these recent research findings...[1]

- The explosive growth in the number of short-term mission (STM) trips among both kids and adults has *not* been accompanied by similarly explosive growth in the number of career missionaries.

- It's not clear whether participation in service trips causes participants to give more money to alleviate poverty once life returns to "normal."

- Participating in a service trip does not seem to reduce participants' tendencies toward materialism.

ARE WE MAKING A DIFFERENCE?

One particularly provocative study led by Dr. Kurt Ver Beek from Calvin College following the devastation of Hurricane Mitch in 1998 challenged many assumptions about the effectiveness of short-term missions. In the study, 40 Hondurans who received new homes from North American STM teams were asked if they would prefer to have

---

1. Robert J. Priest, Terry Dischinger, Steve Rasmussen, and C. M. Brown, "Researching the Short-Term Mission Movement," *Missiology* (34:4, October 2006), 431-50.

the North Americans come and build the homes or be given the $20,000 the short-term groups raised to cover the expense of their trip—an amount that would have enabled the Hondurans to build not just one home but ten. The Hondurans often answered they would rather have the financial resources so they could help *more* families and employ *more* Hondurans.[2]

One Honduran, while very appreciative of the help she received, reported through tears, "It is better for them to send the money in order to help more people who are in need."

Another Honduran leader answered, "They gather money to come here to do work—work that we are capable of doing."

Of course, the Hondurans were also consistently appreciative of all the North Americans had provided for them. Yet their comments leave us wondering: *Are the people we serve really being impacted as deeply as we think they are?*

But if we are really honest, many of us do short-term missions not because of its benefits for those we serve but because we believe it transforms our students. However, Kurt Ver Beek and his team examined 11 factors in the lives of the STM team members (most of whom were adults), including their levels of giving and the time spent volunteering, reading about missions, and praying for missions. In the case of financial giving to the organization that sponsored their trip, 16 percent reported that their giving increased significantly after the trip; 44 percent reported a slight increase in giving; 40 percent reported no increase.[3]

Ver Beek then compared the STMers' impressions of their own giving with the financial records of the missions organizations. According to the records of the sponsoring organizations, only 25 percent of the participants gave anything at all to the missions organization that sponsored their trip. Financial giving to the STMers' own churches increased an average of 1 percent, with six churches experiencing an increase in giving and 11 churches actually receiving less money.[4]

To paraphrase the *Field of Dreams* mantra: If we send them, they will grow...

Maybe.

> To find out more about free research-based resources from the Fuller Youth Institute or to sign up for the free *FYI E-Journal*, visit www.fulleryouthinstitute.org.

THE GOOD NEWS IS ALL THE BETTER

As we come to terms with the bad news that our service is more superficial than we would hope, we're all eager for tools that help us make a deeper impact on our kids and our world. Over the past few years, we at the Fuller Youth Institute (FYI), in collaboration with Dave Livermore of the Global Learning Center at Grand Rapids Theological Seminary and Terry Linhart of Bethel College (Indiana), have helped convene two summits of experts in short-term missions.[5]

---

2. Kurt Ver Beek, "The Impact of Short-Term Missions: A Case Study of House Construction in Honduras after Hurricane Mitch," *Missiology* (34:4, October 2006), 482-83.

3. Of course, financial giving is not the only indicator of whether the needle's tilted toward justice as a lifestyle.

4. Ver Beek, 490. Ver Beek's findings run counter to several previous studies that cite the life-transformation created by STM. Yet critics of previous studies point out that such studies often rely on small sample sizes and are generally done right after the STM trip while participants are still on a "missions high." In addition, previous studies typically have asked participants to rate how their own lives have changed without checking their perceptions against other empirical measures of change. Such self-report data may be biased, as was possibly the case with the 127 STMers who described their increased giving to Ver Beek.

5. We are deeply indebted to our co-researchers Dave Livermore and Terry Linhart for the design and facilitation of these summits, in addition to all the participants who sacrificially gave their time and deep insights: Jared Ayers, George Bache, Noel Becchetti, Terry Bley, Todd Bratulich, Tom Carpenter, Sean Cooper, April Diaz, Brian Dietz, Joel Fay, Hal Hamilton, Brian Heerwagen, Eric Iverson, Tom Ives, Cari Jenkins, Johnny Johnston, Kent Koteskey, Sandy Liu, Mark Maines, Mark Matlock, Daryl Nuss, Derry Prenkert, Rich Van Pelt, Kurt Rietema, David Russell, David Schultz, Bob Whittet, and Kim Williams.

During those summits, we've asked tough questions like:

- How can our service work be part of God's kingdom justice?

- How do we move service beyond spiritual tourism?

- What are the most important theological threads that should weave their way through our service?

- How does service contribute to teenagers' identity development?

- How can we move beyond rhetoric to true partnership with those we're serving?

With the help of some sharp minds and a lot of prayer, we wrestled with those questions and tried to pin down at least some answers. Those answers were translated into 60 learning activities that were field-tested by youth leaders and their students across the country during the spring and summer of 2008. Based on the input we received from youth groups a lot like yours, we revised the book you have in your hands and also developed a parallel student resource, the *Deep Justice Journeys Student Journal*.

THE MODEL IN THE DRIVER'S SEAT

As we searched high and low for research and tools that would increase transformation, one theme repeatedly emerged everywhere we looked: We need to do a better job walking with students before, during, and after their mission experience. [6]

Let's be honest. Our "preparation" before the usual short-term mission trip usually consists of M&Ms: Money and Medical Releases. Our "reflection" during the trip boils down to a few minutes of prayer requests before our team tumbles into bed, exhausted. And our "debrief" after we get home is little more than organizing the media show and the testimonies to share in "big church."

If we want greater transformation, we need a completely different timeframe for our service. Perhaps instead of viewing a weekend trip to work with homeless people in the inner city as a three-day commitment, we need to view it as a three-month process. Instead of looking at a week in the Dominican Republic as seven days, we need to think of it as seven-month journey. Instead of thinking of service as discrete chunks of time we slide in and around the rest of what we do in youth ministry, maybe it's time to revise our schedule to give service a more organic ebb and flow.

---

6. The following section is adapted from an article co-authored by Kara Powell, Dave Livermore, Terry Linhart, and Brad Griffin entitled "If We Send Them, They Will Grow...Maybe" available at www.fulleryouthinstitute.org.

WHAT DO WE DO WITH ALL THAT TIME?

So what do we do with those extra weeks before and after our service experience? And how do we squeeze every ounce of impact out of the time we spend doing missions work?

The many hands and brains that have poured into this curriculum recommend an experiential education framework originally proposed by Laura Joplin[7], and later modified and tested by Terry Linhart[8] on youth STM trips.

THE BEFORE/DURING/AFTER MODEL

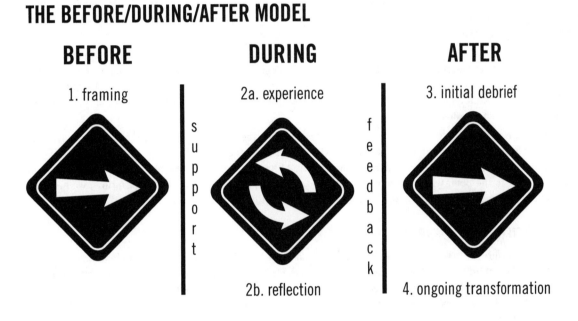

Step 1. BEFORE: *FRAMING*

A successful service or learning experience starts when we help students FRAME the sometimes mind-blowing and other times menial experiences that await them. Getting ready for a mission experience involves much more than just helping them raise money, learn a drama, or know what to pack. Research indicates that our job as youth workers is to facilitate a series of gatherings and events that prepare students emotionally, mentally, spiritually, and relationally for what lies ahead. If we don't, we're cheating them out of all God has for them.

During this framing time, you might want to nudge your students to start journaling about their thoughts and feelings as they think about what lies ahead, and the *Deep Justice Journeys Student Journal* can help you do just that.

---

7. Laura Joplin, "On Defining Experiential Education" in K. Warren, M. Sakofs, and J. S. Hunt Jr. eds., *The Theory of Experiential Education* (Dubuque, IA: Kendall/Hunt Publishing Company, 1995), 15-22.

8. Terrence D. Linhart, "Planting Seeds: The Curricular Hope of Short Term Mission Experiences in Youth Ministry" *Christian Education Journal* (Series 3, 2005), 256-72. For the purposes of this curriculum, some of the terminology in the model has been modified.

Step 2. DURING: *EXPERIENCE AND REFLECTION*

The main component in students' learning during their actual service is the cycle of EXPERIENCE AND REFLECTION. In this ongoing feedback loop, you and your students are placed in situations and activities that purposefully stretch you. Maybe you'll use new skill muscles in a cross-cultural setting unfamiliar to you. Or your group will get tired, cranky, and hungry—and the glue that has united your students up to this point will start to dissolve.

Whatever your students are experiencing, they are constantly assigning meaning. Though they are often unconscious of it, your teenagers are continually engaged in a highly personal, ongoing "conversation" in their own minds about who they are in relation to themselves, others, and God.

The constant barrage of experiences on a typical service adventure come so fast and furious that kids often feel as if they're sprinting through a museum, only barely viewing its masterpieces out of the corners of their eyes. As adult youth workers, our job is to give space for students to catch their breath and ask questions that help decipher the deep meaning behind their observations, thoughts, and feelings.

If you are serving with students who struggle to process their feelings and experiences (can anyone say "middle school boys"?), then your first attempts to help kids reflect on their experiences may get just a few bites of conversation. Answers may range from "I don't know" to "What he said." That's okay. Sometimes it takes months—or years—to get to the point where students are able to truly join in the reflection. In the meantime, we have the opportunity to model patient listening and simply being there with them.

Step 3. AFTER: *INITIAL DEBRIEF*

At the end of your trip, as your students' minds and your ministry's minivans are starting to head home, you've now entered the third step: INITIAL DEBRIEF. Maybe it's the last day of your STM trip as you take a bit of time for R&R. Or perhaps it's when you hit a coffee shop together right after you've visited patients at the local children's hospital. Either way, the goal is to gather your team together after the "work" is completed to start thinking about the even harder work of long-term transformation.

Step 4. AFTER: *ONGOING TRANFORMATION*

If most youth groups lack an effective pre-service framing time, even more have difficulty facilitating proper ONGOING TRANSFORMATION. Two realities fight against effective learning transfer. First, most of the significant growth in a service experience takes place in an environment very different from the home communities of students. Second, the students themselves don't know how to translate the learning to their own lives. That's why we need to help them connect the dots between having lunch with a homeless man in Detroit and having lunch with a new kid in their school cafeteria one month later.

Through it all: *SUPPORT* and *FEEDBACK*

To facilitate the experience-and-reflection cycle, our discussions and activities need to be surrounded by walls of SUPPORT and FEEDBACK. While these two expressions of care are vital throughout the process, their importance peaks during the time you're actually serving.

Sound complicated? It sure is. But offering kids support and feedback through the entire process is essential. See pages 16-20 for more on that.

You might assume support and feedback would flow most naturally from the other adults and students on your team. While that is often true, the best networks stretch far beyond the immediate team. Research shows a strong correlation between individuals' success in a cross-cultural experience and the emotional and tangible support they receive from friends and family. Thus, support can (and, dare we say, often *should*) also include the financial, logistical, and emotional assistance provided by a sending church, denomination group, or STM agency. Plus, let's not forget support from the people in the community we're serving. Many of them can wrap your students in the type of love that both comforts and convicts.

One primary purpose of such feedback is to nudge group members beyond their initial conclusions and help them suspend judgment until they've gone deeper in service. For example, your group may be serving overseas in an under-resourced community plagued by poverty. While there, students may notice a lot of people smiling at them. The "fast" conclusion can be, "Even without much money or stuff, these people are happy." Are they? Maybe—but maybe not. Perhaps the locals are simply being polite. Whatever the case, we might assume the nonverbal behavior we're observing here means the same thing it means at home. Proper feedback helps us avoid becoming knee-jerk experts.

ASSUMPTIONS IN THE PASSENGER'S SEAT

If the model we've just outlined is in the driver's seat, the following assumptions are in the passenger's seat—making suggestions that influence when your group should turn left, when you should turn right, and when you should make a U-turn and head in the opposite direction:

1. **As your students serve, they have opportunities to learn about themselves, their youth group, their God, and their world.** Because of this, both this leader's guide (and the student journal) work through the steps of FRAMING, EXPERIENCE AND REFLECTION, INITIAL DEBRIEF, and ONGOING TRANSFORMATION in three dimensions: GOD AND ME, GOD AND US (meaning the youth group), and GOD AND THE LOCALS (meaning the people we serve). So you can pick and choose exercises that help students grow in their understanding of their lives, their youth group, and their role as world Christians. That reminds us...

2. **A good missions curriculum is easy to use but it's also customizable.** After all, we know students, but we don't know *your* students. We know something about service, but we don't know all the details about *your* upcoming adventure. So while we've given you these learning exercises in an order that feels logical to us and that worked well for the youth groups who tested this curriculum, you might want to pick and choose items off the menu in a different order. You're the expert on the kids and families in your community, and these resources are designed so you can adapt them to what God is doing in and through your service.

3. **The best projects help students move past service to examine the justice issues at the root of the needs they are addressing.** Here's one way to think of the difference between service and social justice: We serve when we give food to people in need; we engage in social justice when we figure out and address why people don't have the food they need, and then work with those folks to change the situation so they can get the food they need in the future. We want to help the students in our ministries dive past service into the deeper, and often murkier, waters of social justice—into places where they can find lasting solutions to systemic problems. Suburban, urban, rural, or something in between, our prayer is that this curriculum helps your ministry dig deeper into the injustices around you so you can unearth the hope

and freedom of the gospel. If you want to discuss this difference with your students, see "The Parable of the Cracked Roads" on pages 30-33.

4. **Smart youth ministries are good at "cultural intelligence."** Virtually every service or STM trip involves cross-cultural relationships in which you interact with folks from a different background, ethnicity, geography, or economic status. As described by Dr. Dave Livermore, one of the contributors to this curriculum, cultural intelligence (or CQ) assumes that you and your students are constantly engaging in a process of observing and responding to cultural cues and encounters. Similar to IQ or EQ (emotional intelligence), your group's CQ is strengthened by the GOD AND LOCALS exercises that help you reach across cultural gaps in ways that are appropriate, respectful, and even—dare we dream?— transformative.[9]

5. **Wise youth leaders know WHY their students are involved in service and justice work.** Before you ask yourself the important questions *(What do we want to do? Where do we want to do it? And how in the world are we going to pay for it?)*, there's a more fundamental question you need to tackle: *Why are you involving your youth ministry in service and justice work?* Because you've always done it? Because other youth ministries do it? Because your students/church leaders/parents/bosses/deacons expect you to do it? Because Jesus expects you to do it? Because your own life was impacted by service and justice work when you were a teenager? Because you want to stretch your kids? Because you want your students to be exposed to the multicultural reality of our world today? Take some time, both on your own and in conversation with the other adults and students on your team, to prayerfully prioritize the main reasons you feel called to extend God's justice to the least, the last, and the lost. (Here's some good news: The learning activity on page 35 helps you and your team pinpoint in just a single sentence why you're doing this work.)

6. **The more students' senses are engaged in learning about service and justice, the better.** Students are visual learners. (We wish we had a video or slideshow to make that point, but ironically, we don't.) Because of that, we've incorporated videos and other experiential elements that involve not just students' ears, but their eyes, noses, fingers, and mouths.

7. **The kids who really "get" service and social justice usually have families who get it also.** Parents generally have more influence with students than youth workers do. Do the math: We're with their kids for a few hours a week and for a handful of years; parents have them the rest of the time and they share life— the good, the bad, and the ugly—with them every day. Because of that, pages 21-26 extend the invitation to serve beyond the inbox of our 16-year-olds. Like pretty much everything else we do in youth ministry, our impact on both the 16-year-old and our planet will be magnified when we do the hard work of adding parents' names to our invitation lists.

8. **Service is a church family affair.** The church family also has an important part to play in students' service. Your church is more than just a group of people to hit up for money or a worship service that gives you 10 minutes to share after your trip. Your church community can be a catalyst for deeper impact. We hope you discuss, and then implement, some of the ideas on pages 27 and 28 with your whole church.

9. **Don't underestimate the power of partnership.** Many youth ministries have found that effective partnerships make the difference between a good service experience and a *great* service experience. While

---

9. See Dave Livermore, *Serving With Eyes Wide Open* (Grand Rapids: Baker, 2006). CQ was initially developed by Soon and Earley in *Cultural Intelligence: Individual Interactions Across Cultures* (Palo Alto, CA: Stanford UP, 2003). Soon and Earley built upon Gardiner's research on multiple intelligences. For a quick tutorial on CQ, see Brad Griffin's article at www.fulleryouthinstitute.org entitled "No Longer an Option: The Essential Role of Cultural Intelligence in Youth Ministry."

much of this book will explore how to develop true partnership with the people you're serving, a second important partner many youth ministries rely upon is an STM agency that helps coordinate the trip. To find out more about how to choose a wise agency partner, check out the Seven U.S. Standards of Excellence in Short-Term Mission at www.stmstandards.org.

10. **Common terms are our friends...sometimes.** As we developed and tested this curriculum, we realized there are some inherent problems with the terminology we often use to describe our efforts. Here are some questions that just wouldn't go away:

   • As we move beyond *service* to justice, what verbs in addition to serve can we use to describe what we do? ("To just" isn't a verb.)

   • Does the word *serve* imply some sort of unequal need? In other words, does such language suggest that the people doing the service are somehow subtly superior to those who receive the service?

   • Does the very term "short-term mission trip" contradict a more holistic vision for viewing missions as a lifestyle?

   In the midst of these tensions, we've tried our best to use language that is both clear and accurate. We're not sure we always succeeded.

HOW TO GET THE MOST OUT OF THIS BOOK

Now we're handing the keys over to you (driver's seat, passenger's seat, now car keys...have we taken the metaphor too far?). How do you get the most out of the pages that follow?

1. **Give your students time and space for their own reflection before, during, and after your justice work.** Based on the feedback we have received from youth workers, we developed the *Deep Justice Journeys Student Journal* as a companion piece to this leader's guide. The journal gives your students an easy space and place to reflect and respond during their personal devotions or in the midst of your team discussions. Plus your students are much more likely to keep their journals for years to come than they are a stack of handouts. Most of—but not all—the exercises in this guide have parallel reflection exercises in the journal.

   By no means do you *need* to purchase a journal for each student. The exercises in this leader's guide are all designed to work just fine without the journal—and, in fact, the journal can also work effectively on its own.

2. **Schedule time to meet with your group before, during, and after you serve.** Don't skimp on this. Even if it means you do two fewer Bible studies or three fewer worship team practices, you and your students will be better off if you give yourself plenty of time to frame, discuss, and debrief your service.

   When we tested this curriculum with youth ministries around the country, a consistent theme in youth workers' feedback was that they weren't used to scheduling meetings *after* their justice work. But when youth workers made the effort to meet with their students afterwards, they felt the seeds God had planted during the actual justice experience went deeper and bore greater fruit.

If you're planning a one-week trip to an urban community two hours away, your journey timeframe might look something like this:

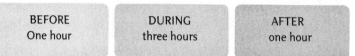

BEFORE	DURING	AFTER
three months	one week	three months

If you're planning a three-hour visit to the local rescue mission, your timeframe might look more like this:

BEFORE	DURING	AFTER
One hour	three hours	one hour

By now, you might be wondering if the Before/During/After Model is something you progress through *once* during the many months involved in your service experience, or if it's something that you progress through *many times*. The answer is BOTH. Part of the beauty of the Before/During/After Model is that you can walk through it in a morning, in a week, or during a yearlong emphasis on service or missions.

3. **Tentatively plan the exercises you'll do during those meetings, being sensitive to the various topics and codes for each exercise.** In order to help you organize your teaching, we've done a bit of organizing for you already:

- GOD AND ME, GOD AND US, GOD AND THE LOCALS. We've already told you about these three content categories that weave their way throughout the entire book.

- THE ORDER OF THE EXERCISES. The exercises placed earlier in each section of the book (Before, During, and After) often lay groundwork for future exercises. Since you probably won't be able to complete all the exercises in any one section during a single justice mission, you might want to focus your attention on those placed first. But obviously, you know your kids and your project better than we do, so please flip through all the exercises before zeroing in.

- INTEGRATING SCRIPTURE. Some exercises are "No Scripture," others are "Some Scripture," and still others are "Lotsa Scripture."

LOTSA SCRIPTURE

- TIME. Most exercises can be done in 20 to 40 minutes. For those of you who prefer longer discussions, we've marked additional ideas as HAVE MORE TIME?

DEVOTION friendly

DEVOTION FRIENDLY. Since many of you will want to lead daily group devotions with your students or give them time with God on their own, we've marked five exercises in the DURING section that can easily be used for this purpose with the icon just to the left of this paragraph. If your students are using the *Deep Justice Journeys Student Journal*, you can direct them to exercises for their personal reflection or group discussion. Otherwise, you will probably need to give some verbal instructions, make copies of the handouts in this book, and/or point students to the relevant Scripture passages so they can reflect and pray on their own.

We are thrilled to be navigating these deep justice journeys with you. It's time to buckle up our youth ministries and enjoy the kingdom ride!

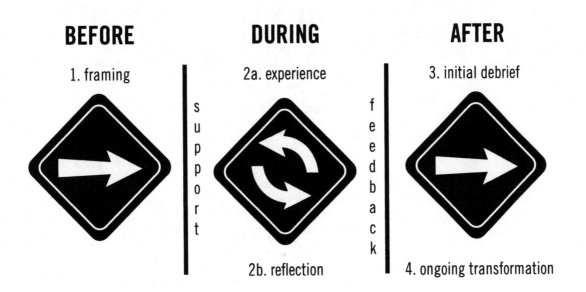

BEFORE

1. framing

DURING

2a. experience

2b. reflection

AFTER

3. initial debrief

4. ongoing transformation

support

feedback

This model is built upon an experiential education framework originally proposed by Laura Joplin, and later modified and tested by Terry Linhart on youth ministry short-term mission trips. See Joplin, 15-22, and Linhart, 256-72. For the purposes of this curriculum, some of the terminology in the model has been modified.

JOURNEYING TOGETHER: CREATING WALLS OF SUPPORT AND FEEDBACK FOR STUDENTS

BY BRAD GRIFFIN

I recently shared a short-term mission trip with 14-year-old Amanda from our church. Amanda stood out because she walked into our trip more obviously broken than most kids, and seemed more than a little hesitant about the cross-cultural realities we faced every day. To be honest, I was more than a little hesitant about her, and not long into the trip I heard another leader mention that Amanda seemed really disengaged.

But Amanda didn't walk alone through her experience. Laura was there, too—an adult who had been Amanda's small-group leader and was intentionally tracking with Amanda during this trip.

Our work was focused around teaching sustainable micro-gardening in our host community—not overtly spiritual stuff. I didn't have great confidence in the transformative potential of this experience for Amanda. Yet the night before we packed up to head home, Amanda shared about a profound faith experience. The previous evening Amanda had talked with God. She'd lain awake for several hours praying and wrestling with God's presence in all she'd seen and experienced—and then offered her life to God. She confessed to us that she was anxious about what that might mean for her back at home. Our team prayed with her, reminding her she was not alone in her faith journey.

Two months later, Amanda stood in front of our congregation and shared about God's movement in her life before and since that trip, and was baptized as a public declaration of her faith in Christ. But Amanda didn't make that declaration alone, either; Laura was there with her, participating in Amanda's baptism. And we were there, too—adults and students who pledged to keep walking with Amanda.

Amanda's story represents two fundamental pieces of the short-term missions puzzle: *Support* and *feedback*. Laura consistently offered Amanda a sounding board for her questions, and our team provided a safe place for her to be vulnerable about her stumble into faith. Back home, friends at church and our youth pastor added further pieces to the puzzle, voicing their encouragement and being patient with her struggles.

As we explained in the previous section (pages 6-15), the model behind these deep justice journeys is the experiential education framework originally proposed by Laura Joplin,[11] and later modified and tested by Terry Linhart.[12] In the center of the model is a cycle (Joplin pictured it as a hurricane) of challenging experience paired with reflection.

---

11. Joplin, 15-22.

12. Linhart, 256-72. For the purposes of this curriculum, some of the terminology in the model has been modified.

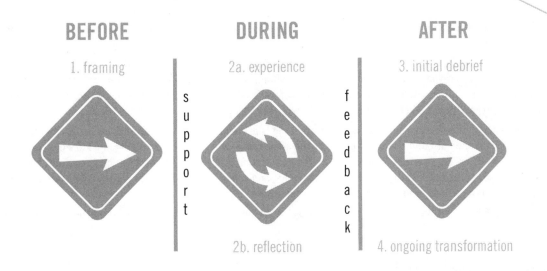

Note that this cycle of experience and reflection does not exist in a vacuum. Surrounding experience and reflection are *support* and *feedback*, two parallel walls that hold up the process. Support provides safety for students to keep trying even when they flounder, and feedback helps students form appropriate judgments and offers new insights to their experiences along the way.

Here's how it works: As kids are being purposefully stretched by their encounters on your justice journey, they are constantly assigning internal meaning to those experiences. The conversations in their heads never stop as their brains work overtime to process the often-disjointed perspectives of reality they tumble through each day. While the goals of *reflection* and *debrief* are to help decipher these messages and give them lasting meaning, *support* and *feedback* provide the backdrop for this whole drama. As it unfolds, trusted adults are somewhat like stage managers, giving cues and offering encouragement.

SETTING UP SCAFFOLDING

Lev Vygotsky (pronounced vuh-GOT-skee) was a developmental theorist who studied the social processes of development in children and adolescents. Vygotsky developed two interrelated concepts that help us think more deeply about support and feedback: *Zone of proximal development* and *scaffolding*.[13]

The **zone of proximal development** refers to a range of tasks and concepts that are just beyond a student's current field of mastery, for which they need some assistance from another person to learn. So in the case of a student on a justice journey, this zone could include anything from installing drywall to working with young children to sharing one's faith in front of a group (and in the case of many justice journeys, all three challenges in the same week!). But rather than depending entirely on that student's personal competence, intelligence, or grit to figure this stuff out, Vygotsky asserts that *relationships* are the key to building skills in this zone. It's through relationships with

---

13. Vygotsky's work is well-described and illustrated by Jack O. Balswick, Pamela E. King, and Kevin S. Reimer in *The Reciprocating Self: Human Development in Theological Perspective* (Downers Grove: InterVarsity Press, 2005), 90-97.

adults that kids gain the support they need to safely explore and tackle tasks just beyond their mental, physical, or emotional reach.

Similarly, *scaffolding* serves as the safe structure around the emerging adolescent that supports growth and fosters co-learning with adults and other kids. Just as scaffolding on a building allows workers access to each part of the structure as it rises, adults become the steadying force that is carefully added (when kids are most in need of that support) and removed (when they need to be set free to try on their own).

Please don't miss the imagery here: Just as scaffolding is made up of many interlocking pieces in order to balance the weight and surround the building, so no one adult can provide all the scaffolding in a kid's life. To truly thrive, every adolescent needs an interlocking network of caring adults. In STM and justice encounters, this is especially true. In the midst of experiences that challenge and stretch them, kids need safe people and places to support the overwhelming amount of processing taking place.

Keeping this imagery in mind, below are a few tips for building webs of support under kids as they stretch their justice wings:

1. Maximize Support Channels.

One mistake we often make when creating support structures around students is failing to capture the potential available to us. Support can take many shapes and sizes, and part of our role as leaders is to maximize this network for our students before, during, and after the justice journey.

Support can come from other people sharing in the experience—other students on the team, adults, local hosts—or it can come via the church family back home. Support comes in multiple forms, including finances and prayer as well as verbal and emotional footings. Knowing that their community has invested money, trust, and prayer into the ministry of their team is an incredible witness of God's faithfulness to kids in the midst of their justice work.

We also limit the support channels provided for students when we cling to a narrow perspective of who makes a "good" adult volunteer on a mission trip. As in other aspects of youth ministry, youth workers often look for only the youngest and hippest prospects to help lead justice experiences. But in following this strategy, we may miss out on folks who bring not only different life experiences, but also a different level of safety for students.

Grandparents are one example. It had never occurred to me to invite grandparents along on a student mission trip until Julie asked if hers could join us for two weeks in Costa Rica. In many ways Bob and Jean were the heroes of that trip. They offered an ultra-safe presence to kids and adults alike, and their years of wisdom steadied us without smothering us. Don't be afraid to step outside the realm of "normal" when you begin to build a support team for your next justice-oriented trip—you might be surprised by who you find ready to journey alongside your students!

2. Create Opportunities for Risk.

Whole books have been written about learning through our failures, so we probably don't need to convince you of that. But as leaders we sometimes forget to allow kids opportunities to risk failure as part of the learning process.

Our role as adults giving support and feedback includes creating space for risk. In order to be willing to step into a space of risk, kids have to feel safe. One of my early mentors in leading wilderness trips trained us to continually assess where participants fall on the *OSV* scale as a way to gauge our environment for healthy risk-taking. *OSV* stands for *Oriented, Safe, and Valued*. I encourage adult leaders to periodically ask (sometimes out loud, but often internally):

1. *Is each person oriented?* Does he understand where we are, where we're headed, and what's going on?

2. *Does each person feel safe?* Physically, emotionally, spiritually, and mentally, have we pushed too far beyond the bounds of comfort for anyone (or everyone)?

3. *Does each person feel valued?* Have we communicated in any way that anyone's voice is not important or that her safety doesn't matter? Have we devalued the image of God in anyone by our actions, words, or attitudes?

These three simple guidelines help us assess whether we are creating safe and supportive environments for students to take healthy risks as they interact cross-culturally and make efforts to serve others.

3. Reflect Back What You See.

As kids dive into cross-cultural experiences or take on near-heroic tasks ("Let's build a house in a week!"), they need accurate information about not only what they're *seeing* but also what they're *doing*. Sometimes the most important insights you can share with a student are your observations about how that person is working, interacting with others, or exhibiting particular character traits.

When reflecting, it is important to be as specific as possible. It's more valuable to hear, "Tim, your encouraging comment to Sandy about the way she led games with the kids showed real selflessness, especially since you'd wanted to be the game leader," than to hear, "Tim, you're a really nice guy."

4. Level the Playing Field.

Feedback is best received when there is what Joplin calls an "equalization of power" between the participant and the leader. This doesn't mean we should negate our leadership in the midst of stretching experiences, but it might mean revisiting how we lead during those moments.

Kids will be more likely to hear and apply our feedback when we *share power* with them as much as possible. This might mean we bring a few students into the decision-making meetings about the work project at hand. It might also mean we spend as little time as possible during our trip doing "leader-type" things and way more time doing servant jobs. When kids see us digging the sewage drain, mixing the concrete, or washing the dishes after a meal, they gain a new perspective on what it means to lead. Such leveling of the playing field often renders students more likely to hear us when we offer the feedback they so desperately need in the midst of their work.

WHAT SUPPORT IS NOT

Recently a friend told me about a mom and son she'd seen at an airport. They were eating, and the son was being spoon-fed by his mother. But the boy was not an infant—he was an early adolescent, perfectly capable of feeding himself. His mom was feeding him because the young man was too busy playing a video game to stop and eat lunch. Seriously.

That mom needs some help with boundaries. And perhaps she needs help understanding the difference between support and, well, perpetuating immaturity. In other words support is *not* an escape hatch for reluctant young fledglings to duck back in the nest and hide, comfortably sucking on worms. It's more like a safety net 10 branches down, carefully positioned to catch if necessary, but only after the little bird has actually jumped and stretched its wings a bit.

During your justice journey you (or other adults on your team) might find it tempting to bail kids out whenever they hit a challenging moment, a cultural wall, or the consequences of a bad decision. While there are certainly times we should bail out our students—especially if their or others' safety is jeopardized—we must walk a fine line between being the safety net and being the spoon-feeding parent.

THE RECOVERY TENT

If you've ever been part of a long-distance running race, you're probably familiar with the "recovery tent." Race planners with any kind of experience know that once runners hit the finish line, all kinds of (often painful) things can happen to their bodies and minds—cramping, nausea, disorientation, chills, and sometimes even more drastic experiences like heart failure. So the recovery tent was designed to supply post-race athletes with appropriate food, foil blankets, lots of water, and medical attention.

In a similar way, after a day—or a week, or three weeks—of serving cross-culturally, students need a recovery-tent environment to catch their breath, find some nourishment, and attend to their wounds. We have the *responsibility* to build a team of trusted adults who can create that type of recovery-tent environment around the students in our care. When we do, the Amandas on our teams will have opportunities to experience something significant in the recovery tent at the end of the day. Hopefully it will be one of the ways our kids will come face-to-face with God during their journeys.

PARENTS: MORE THAN CHECKBOOKS AND CHAUFFEURS

BY KARA POWELL

If you're like most of us in youth ministry, where do you turn when you need money to fund your service events? Your students' parents.

Who do you assume will transport your students to and from your justice work? Their parents.

While it's great to have the financial backing of your students' families, and we all love those families that let us borrow their big SUVs for service events, deeper justice will come only when we view parents as more than just checkbooks and chauffeurs.

One of the best ways to partner with parents in deeper justice is to empower them through good communication. Let's take some time to think about how we can most effectively engage with parents BEFORE, DURING, and AFTER a mission experience…

BEFORE: THE PRE-SERVICE PARENT MEETING

We encourage you to schedule a 90-minute meeting with students and their parents near the very start of your pre-service events and training meetings. Make sure you set a warm and friendly tone by arranging your chairs in a circle and offering *adult* snacks (meaning more than a bag of crushed tortilla chips and some stale M&Ms).

There will invariably be students whose parents cannot (or don't want to) come. Please let these students know they are welcome to invite another adult, and if that doesn't work out, you can play the part of their parent for the evening.

You'll need:

- Copies of the Before/During/After Model (page 15) Parent Covenant handout (page 24)
- Pencils or pens
- Poster paper
- Markers

Before the meeting begins, hang four large pieces of poster paper along the walls of your meeting space. Write one of the following four headers on each piece of paper: KIDS' DREAMS FOR THEMSELVES, PARENTS' DREAMS FOR THEMSELVES, OUR DREAMS FOR OUR FAMILY AND OUR CHURCH FAMILY, and OUR DREAMS FOR THOSE WE SERVE.

At some point in this (or another) meeting, make sure you provide a thorough description of your work's logistics, including:

- Why you chose this place for your service

- Your partners (any agencies or churches with whom you're working)

- What you'll actually be doing during your justice work

- Food and lodging arrangements

- Funding needed and the amount each student/family is expected to contribute

- Fundraising strategies and how students and families are expected to participate

- Transportation

- Safety precautions

- Medical release forms and insurance (health or otherwise) needed

- What students need to bring with them

- A schedule of additional meetings both before and after your service

Once people arrive, welcome everyone and ask the students to introduce their parent(s). Depending on the level of vulnerability in the group, you might ask students to share something unusual about their parents or one thing they've appreciated about their parents recently.

Ask parents: **Why are you excited for your kids to be part of our upcoming service experience?**

After several parents have answered, explain: **Many folks in churches (not our church, of course, but other churches!) tend to think that when it comes to service, something is better than nothing. In other words, any service is better than no service. I wish that were the case, but it's not.** Share some of the relevant research insights described in the "Initial Steps" section of this curriculum (pages 6-7).

Explain: **As someone who wants to ensure that our service work makes a lasting impression on these students, on our church, and on the locals we'll be partnering with, I'm pleased to say we are working diligently on a deeper approach to our service work.** At this point, distribute copies of the Before/During/After Model found on page 15. Walk students and parents through the method, drawing from the explanation given on pages 8-11 of this curriculum. Along the way, share examples of ways you're planning to engage students in *framing, reflecting, initial debrief,* and *ongoing transformation.*

Continue: **But we can't do this without you. In every aspect of your kids' growth and discipleship—including this one—we want to partner with you. I've shared with you the steps we as a youth ministry are planning in order to deepen the impact of this service on your kids and on the world. Now I'm hoping you'll think tangibly about your own role in our ministry's work for deeper justice.** Distribute copies of the *Parent Covenant* on page 24 and pens to the parents. Make sure to point out that parents can either give specific goals ("I will pray for your service project every day for five minutes") or more general goals ("As I think of this upcoming service, I will pray for you all"). You definitely don't want to create an atmosphere of competition among parents, or to cause parents to think they'll somehow be judged based on their level of commitment. We recommend that you let parents keep their copy of the *Parent Covenant* after they've filled it out, so you don't even see what they've written. Hopefully parents will feel comfortable sharing their covenant commitments with their own kids, either right now or later on.

The "post-service support" category in the handout is one you should think about ahead of time. How do you hope parents will stay engaged after the justice work? At the very minimum, we strongly encourage you to schedule a 60-minute post-event meeting for students and parents (see pages 25-26). In addition, you can invite students and parents to other *ongoing transformation* activities you will plan. Share as much detail as possible about those post-service activities now—so parents can think about and write down what they'd like to commit to.

After parents are finished, explain: **I'd like us to close our meeting by taking some time to dream and pray. As you can see, we've hung four different sheets of poster paper around the room. The first says KIDS' DREAMS FOR THEMSELVES. I'd like students to walk up to this paper and use markers and write out (or draw) their dreams for how our service will impact them.**

The second poster paper says PARENTS' DREAMS FOR THEMSELVES. As you can probably guess, I'd like parents to use markers to write out (or draw) on this sheet their hopes for how the youth ministry's service will impact them as parents. You might want to give a few examples of the type of dreams parents could write, such as praying for God to do great work and then celebrate the answered prayers with their kids, or being more informed and involved in issues of poverty and justice. (Note: In order to avoid bottlenecks, you might hang up multiple sheets of poster paper for each category.)

After students and parents have finished writing their dreams on their poster papers, have them huddle as families for a few minutes to share what they've written.

Once the families have finished sharing what they wrote on the first two sheets of poster paper, explain the next stage of the process: **Now I'd like to invite you to move together as a family to the last two sheets of poster paper labeled OUR DREAMS FOR OUR FAMILY AND OUR CHURCH FAMILY and OUR DREAMS FOR THOSE WE SERVE. On each piece of paper, please write (or draw) the ways you hope this service impacts your family and our church, as well as the people you'll be serving. These might be new dreams that will hopefully emerge from the service, or they might be dreams you're already pursuing that hopefully the service will fuel.** Here again, you might want to give some examples. A family might hope to sponsor a child or a family through monthly donations or more diligently cleaning out closets and donating clothes and household items to those who are poor. Dreams for those we serve might include providing new venues for ongoing education or creating job skills and greater job-placement opportunities.

Give plenty of time for families to write on all four sheets of poster paper and then close in prayer. You can close in prayer as a group (perhaps even holding hands and inviting parents to pray for the youth ministry's service) or you can ask each family to huddle and pray together.

Make sure you save all four pieces of poster paper. They will come in handy during your post-service parent meeting.

Having heard the work and energy the youth ministry leadership is devoting to the upcoming service experience, I would like to commit to the following (please write a goal for any appropriate categories):

PRAYER SUPPORT (e.g., committing to pray daily for my student's justice journey; inviting others to pray on their own or join with me for particular prayer times)

LOGISTICAL SUPPORT (e.g., driving my kid to meetings; trying to avoid schedule conflicts with meetings)

FINANCIAL SUPPORT (e.g., give a certain amount of money before, during, or after my student's service work)

COMMUNICATION SUPPORT (e.g., staying on top of communication from the youth ministry; sharing my own thoughts and concerns directly with youth ministry leadership)

POST-SERVICE SUPPORT (e.g., helping your student figure out how to be involved in justice work at home; engaging in justice work as a family)

DURING: SIMPLE BUT STRATEGIC IDEAS THAT ENGAGE PARENTS

While your energy during your actual service will be focused on your kids and the locals you're serving, don't make the all-too-common mistake of neglecting parents. Here are a few simple but strategic ideas to engage parents during your service work:

1. Encourage parents to gather together to serve in your community while your team is serving elsewhere. Then be intentional to have parents and students share about their experiences afterward.

2. During your service experience, invite parents to meet together at your church or a home to pray for your group regularly—maybe even daily.

3. Create a voice mail account with an outgoing message that you (or a student) change with daily updates and highlights.

4. Depending on the technology you have available, provide a forum in which students can send e-mail to parents and vice versa. Or designate a contact parent who will receive e-mails and pass them on.

5. If you have video-conference technology available, invite parents to come together and "call" your group so families can reunite through video.

6. Consider inviting some parents to come along as leaders (check with their kids first to gauge how comfortable they are with this).

7. Create a team blog in which you load daily photos and reflections, and parents can comment with prayers and encouragement.

AFTER: THE POST-SERVICE PARENT MEETING

When meetings for parents are held after a service experience, many youth workers find that few parents attend—and those who do come are usually the parents who are already committed to the type of conversations you're hoping to facilitate. (In other words, they're the ones who least need such a meeting.)

Given that, it's tempting to give up trying to engage with parents after the service. Please resist that temptation.

Hopefully you were able to announce your plans for post-service activities when you held your pre-service parent meeting, and parents were able to commit to those activities in their *Parent Covenant*. Even if that's not the case, we encourage you to consider the following ideas for engaging parents after the activity:

- Give some time for students to write letters to parents during your initial debrief and mail those letters to the parents with an accompanying letter from you that celebrates all the Lord (and the kids!) did.

- Invite parents to some, or all, of your *ongoing transformation* activities after your justice work.

- Schedule a local parent/student service activity in which your students and their families can serve side-by-side.

- Give each parent a copy of any media presentations (e.g., videos, slide shows, PowerPoint presentations) you make.

- Plan a one-hour post-service parent meeting.

As you might guess from the heading for this section, we're big fans of post-service parent meetings. If you followed the pre-service parent meeting suggestions earlier in this chapter, you saved the four sheets of poster paper full of students', parents', and families'/church family dreams, which will be great catalysts for discussion now.

Schedule your post-service parent meeting at a time convenient for students and families. Right after the church's weekly worship service is often a prime time. If possible, serve snacks or a meal to set a festive and positive tone (nothing sets a negative tone like grumbling stomachs).

You'll need:

- The poster papers from the pre-service meeting where students and parents listed dreams for the students, parents, families and church family, and the community being served

Welcome folks and then ask students to introduce their parents. As part of the introductions, you might invite parents to share what they were doing while their kid(s) were off serving.

Explain: **Hopefully by now you parents have had a chance to hear how the Lord worked in and through our youth ministry as we served—at least from the perspective of your own son or daughter. Let's take some time to compare some of our early dreams for ourselves with what actually happened.**

One at a time, invite students to find their own writing (or drawing) on the poster paper marked STUDENTS' DREAMS FOR THEMSELVES and read aloud what they wrote. Ask each student to comment on how those dreams matched, or didn't match, what really happened.

After all students have finished, ask the parents: **What themes did you hear in our students?**

Q: **What, if anything, surprised you about what students shared?**

Explain: **Now it's time for the parents. Instead of doing this as a group, we'll do this sharing as families. Parents, I'd like you to find the dreams you had for yourselves from this poster paper labeled PARENTS' DREAMS FOR THEMSELVES and then huddle up with your kids to talk together about how those initial dreams matched, or didn't match, what really happened.**

After families have completed that discussion, ask them to find what they wrote on the poster papers labeled OUR DREAMS FOR OUR FAMILY AND OUR CHURCH FAMILY and OUR DREAMS FOR THOSE WE SERVE and discuss if those dreams still seem to fit. What new dreams might they have for themselves, the church, and the locals that emerged from, or were fueled by, the service? If they want to add to or revise their dreams, they can feel free to, if necessary, cross out what they originally wrote, and re-write (or re-draw) their new dreams.

Once families are finished, go around the group and ask each family to share one dream they wrote for their family and/or your church family as part of a closing prayer. After each family has finished, the rest of the group should say a one-sentence prayer out loud: "By the grace of our God, may it be so."

YOUR CHURCH: MORE THAN JUST "ISN'T THAT SWEET…?"

BY KARA POWELL

For many youth ministries, the sum total of the church's support of your justice journey is to patiently listen to a few student testimonies and then murmur, "Isn't that sweet…?" Moving beyond this shallow (and somewhat patronizing) level of church engagement takes thought, perseverance, and a bit of diplomacy on your part. While we realize that your church's exposure to your justice work is somewhat beyond your control (we don't know too many churches in which the youth pastor calls the shots), here are some ideas to catapult you and your students into a deeper relationship with your congregation.

LOTSA SCRIPTURE

BEFORE

- Meet with your church's missions committee so its members understand the goals of your service. You may want to invite a few students to attend the meeting with you.

- Ask your senior pastor if you can invite the church to pray for you and your students. Provide a list of specific prayer requests and pictures of your students in your church bulletin.

- Find out about any missionaries or leaders your church already supports in the region you're serving so you can connect with them before and during your justice work.

- Figure out creative ways to invite the congregation to support your trip financially. Some churches have started selling $25 or $50 "shares" congregation members can buy as a way to invest in students' transformation.

- Ask the pastor who works most closely with the children in your church if your students can pair up with one or more children and ask those children to pray for them. Make sure your high school students bring a small gift back for those children.

- Meet with your senior adult ministry and do the same thing.

- Invite a pastor from the community in which you're serving to come to your church and give a five-minute profile, or even an entire sermon, on their community.

- Ask your church or specific Sunday school classes to volunteer to mentor your students. See *Mentoring for Justice* (page 40) for ideas on how to help those mentors connect in meaningful ways with your students.

DURING

- Any Sunday you're gone, give some sort of report at church services through phone calls, video conference calls, or e-mails (depending on the technology available).

- Ask adult classes and small groups to spend a few minutes praying for your justice ministry. (When you get back, be sure to let them know how God answered their prayers!)

- At any church gatherings or services while you're gone, see if the parents of one or two of your students can lead your congregation in prayer.

- Find out any prayer gatherings occurring during your service experience and ask the leaders to pray specifically for your students.

AFTER

- Make sure you report the work God did in and through your students to the entire church. When you share, be sure to highlight what you learned from the people in the community where you served.

- Teach your church any worship songs you learned from the locals.

- Invite the locals you served to share (in person or by video) how God is working in their community and how your group participated in God's work.

- Give the locals cameras and ask them to take pictures of the impact of your service work and share those with your entire congregation.

- Invite adults who can help your students become justice advocates back home to meet with your students. There might be a city council member or community leader in your church; if not, someone in your church is likely to know that type of leader.

- Set up a meeting in which the students and adults who participated in the trip can discuss the experience with your church missions committee. Make sure the agenda includes discussing next steps for the church's participation in this or other justice work.

BEFORE:
FRAMING

Preparing students—and yourself—for all
that awaits you in your journey...

THE PARABLE OF THE CRACKED ROADS

BY KARA POWELL

NO SCRIPTURE

BIG IDEA: Beyond meeting immediate physical needs, justice invites deeper, more holistic, and more systemic solutions.

YOU'LL NEED:

- Whiteboard or poster paper
- Pens
- Bibles
- Copies of **The Parable of the Cracked Roads** handout (pages 32-33), and/or copies of the *Deep Justice Journeys Student Journal* (pages 12-14.) You need at least three copies for your three readers, or you can make copies for everyone.
- HAVE MORE TIME? option: Copies of the **Not-As-Deep Service vs. Deep Justice** handout on page 34

Ideally, you would lead this discussion in a location where cracked roads or cracked concrete is visible (a parking lot, quiet side street, or a deteriorating sidewalk would work well). If that's not possible, you might want to start by commenting on either the cracked roads you've driven on that day or the cracked roads that crisscross their way through your home city.

Ask for three volunteers who like to read aloud and give each one a copy of **The Parable of the Cracked Roads** handout. Explain that each reader represents a different way youth ministries serve others.

After the three readers are finished, lead the following discussion, taking notes on the whiteboard:

Q: **How would you describe the Quick-and-Easy Physical Solution of the first youth ministry?**

Q: **How about the second youth ministry's Warm-and-Fuzzy Friendly Solution?**

Q: **You guessed it...What about the third youth ministry's Deep Solution?**

Q: **Chances are good that the goal of our upcoming mission isn't to fix cracked roads, so let's translate this parable to what we will be doing. What are the immediate physical needs of the people we'll be serving?**

Q: **How will we try to meet those needs?**

Q: Let's think about some deeper needs of the people we've served. What are their...

Emotional needs?

Relational needs?

Educational needs?

Spiritual needs?

Q: What deeper structural problems might have led to those needs?

Q: What is preventing the locals from meeting those needs themselves?

Q: What, if anything, could we do to meet those needs?

Explain: **One way to think about the difference between service and social justice is that we** *serve* **when we give water to people in need; we engage in** *social justice* **when we figure out why those folks don't have the water they need in the first place, and then work with those individuals and communities so they have access to clean water in the future.**

At this point, invite the third reader to re-read the final portion of the parable and then ask: **What would it take for us to move in the direction of the Deep Solution?**

Q: **What would we gain by trying to go deeper? What would we lose?**

Q: **What would it look like if our goal wasn't to meet the needs of the locals, but to help them discover ways to meet their own needs?**

Q: **Chances are good we won't be able to finish the Deep Solution before we head back home. How does that make you feel?**

Q: **What, if anything, can we do once we're back home to help the locals in the area we visited keep making progress toward a Deep Solution?**

Close by giving students a few minutes by themselves to pray individually about the questions and feelings that have emerged as they've contemplated asking the deeper WHY questions. If it doesn't feel safe to send out students as individuals, ask them to sit together, or walk together, but to remain in silent prayer.

HAVE MORE TIME?

Distribute copies of the **Not-As-Deep Service vs. Deep Justice** handout (page 34) to your students and review it together. Lead the following discussion:

Q: **Which parts of the table don't make sense to you?**

Q: **Which rows on the table seem most important for us to keep in mind in our upcoming work? Why?**

Q: **What can we do during our trip to help us be more like the right-hand side of the table?**

Q: **What can we do here at home, both before and after our trip?**

THE PARABLE OF THE CRACKED ROADS

▶ PAGE 1 ◀

READER ONE:

Once upon a time, three youth ministries decided to address an unusual—and dire—problem permeating_____. (Note to reader: Insert the name of the city or town in which you'll be serving.) Somehow, the streets and sidewalks in this town had fallen prey to alarming cracks that crisscrossed the entire town. These cracks were two to four inches wide and several feet long, making the roads dangerous and virtually undrivable. No one knew the exact cause of the cracks, yet residents felt trapped in their homes and ventured to work, school, and church only when necessary.

In an effort to fix the town's problem, the first youth ministry surveyed the damage and came up with a Quick-And-Easy Physical Solution. Their plan was to use a thin layer of topcoat to cover the cracks and render the roads drivable and the sidewalks walkable. Residents stood and watched as the adult leaders and kids poured out of their minivans, mixed up the topcoat, and spread it across the cracks like a layer of chocolate icing on a cake. Pleased with the quick repair, the townfolk hugged the kids and cheered as the youth ministry drove off in minivans.

The topcoat worked.

For a few weeks.

But the weight of the cars, the heat of the sun, and the pounding of the rain soon eroded the topcoat. The cracks reappeared, and residents retreated again to their homes. Some thought the cracks were not as severe as they'd been before the topcoat, but no one could be sure.

READER TWO:

The second youth ministry, after examining the town's broken roads, adopted a different strategy. Recognizing that there was a lot they didn't know, the students figured they'd better learn more about their town's needs and neighbors before making things right. They divided up into teams, some interviewing the residents and others visiting home improvement stores to learn about the type of cement that would best address the problem.

The neighbors had ideas for road repairs that the youth ministry never would have thought of. As a result, the youth ministry was able to develop a Warm-and-Fuzzy Friendly Solution in which the youth ministry and the neighbors worked side by side filling in the cracks with a customized cement.

The cement worked. For six whole months. But then, to the students' dismay, a new series of cracks began to crisscross the roads. Their new friends told them that even though the Warm-and-Fuzzy Friendly Solution had fixed the old cracks, an entirely new set of cracks had emerged, making the roads almost as hazardous.

CONTINUED ON NEXT PAGE >>

Adapted from Chap Clark and Kara E. Powell, *Deep Justice in a Broken World* (Grand Rapids: Zondervan, 2008), 11-12.

READER THREE:

The third youth ministry, having heard about the first two well-intentioned-but-failed strategies, knew that neither topcoat nor a brand new cement would make things right. Like those in the second youth ministry, these students spent several days interviewing neighbors and hearing stories and dreams about crack-free driving as well as the pain and fear caused by the unsafe conditions. Wanting to avoid the mistakes of the first two youth ministries, the third youth ministry adopted a more radical repair strategy.

The students decided to divide into two teams. The first team was tasked with repairing the current cracks. Recognizing that the very foundation of the city's roads was not right, the team members worked with their new friends to jackhammer large sections of road, dig up the resulting rubble, re-level the foundations, and then lay a brand new asphalt surface for the roads.

In order to prevent the cracks from reappearing, the second team investigated a few deeper and more complex questions. First, the kids looked into why the faulty roads had been built in the first place, and lobbied at City Hall to change the construction code so defective roads would never be built again. Second, they asked the local people why they'd been unable to fix the roads, and raised funds to provide the training in construction and asphalt-laying that their neighbors would need to keep the roads shipshape in the future.

This Deep Solution did the trick. Thanks to the new, stable foundation and the neighbors' new training, the broken roads were fixed—for good.

NOT-AS-DEEP SERVICE VS. DEEP JUSTICE

Not-As-Deep Service

Service makes us feel like a "great savior" who rescues the broken.

Service often dehumanizes (even if only subtly) those who are labeled the "receivers."

Service is something we do *for* others.

Service is an event.

Service expects results immediately.

The goal of service is to help others.

Service focuses on what our own ministry can accomplish.

Deep Justice

Justice means God does the rescuing, but often he works through the united power of his great and diverse community to do it.

Justice restores human dignity by creating an environment in which all involved "give" and "receive" in a spirit of reciprocal learning and mutual ministry.

Justice is something we do *with* others.

Justice is a lifestyle.

Justice hopes for results sometime soon but recognizes that systemic change takes time.

The goal of justice is to remove obstacles so others can help themselves.

Justice focuses on how we can work with other ministries to accomplish even more.

Adapted from Chap Clark and Kara E. Powell, *Deep Justice in a Broken World* (Grand Rapids: Zondervan, 2008), 15-16.

NO-BRAINERS

BY BRAD GRIFFIN

BIG IDEA: There are a lot of reasons youth ministries engage in service projects, mission trips, and other kinds of justice work. Early on in your experience, your group should determine exactly why you're going, and state that reason in one clear sentence you can share with others.

SOME
SCRIPTURE

YOU'LL NEED:

- The CD or a copy of the MP3 of "Two Weeks in Africa," a song by Caedmon's Call from the 2007 album *Overdressed*, and a way to play the song for students

- Copies of the **Two Weeks in Africa** handout on page 39 or a way to project the song lyrics for everyone to see, and/or copies of the *Deep Justice Journeys Student Journal* (pages 18-20).

- Poster paper and markers. Ahead of time, tape pieces of poster paper on different walls around the room.

Start by saying, **Most of us do things every day that we simply don't put much thought into. We might call them "no-brainers"—we just do them, seemingly without even thinking. For example, brushing our teeth, putting on deodorant (hopefully!), breathing, and tying our shoes.**

Think for a minute about something you've always done, but you're not really sure why or when you started. Would anyone like to share one of those no-brainers with us?

Q: **Why do we do those things thoughtlessly?**

Q: **Can you think of things we do pretty thoughtlessly that we probably should think harder about?**
   One example for high school students might be driving: We often drive on mental "cruise control" when we really should fully engage our minds and senses before we get behind the wheel of a car.

As we get ready for our upcoming service work, we need to be careful that this experience is not just another no-brainer. If you have not yet defined *justice* with your students, you can do so now by describing it as the way we right wrongs or injustices around us. **Preparing and entering our justice mission on cruise control could lead to a number of negative outcomes: We might get frustrated with one another, ourselves, and our hosts; we might do more harm than good in our host community; and we might not experience the transformation we hope for through this experience—either for ourselves or for the community we're serving.**

Today we're going to take some time to guard against a no-brainer approach to preparing for our mission together. We're taking some time to get at an important question: *Why are we going?* At this point, invite your students to walk around the room and write on the poster paper the reasons they are involved in this justice work.

There are, of course, a number of reasons groups do short-term missions, and even more reasons why individual students choose to go. Some of the reasons students list might include: We've always gone, other youth ministries do it, my own previous experience, church leaders/parents expect it, to be stretched or changed, multicultural exposure, to bring justice where we see injustice, to serve the poor, to be with friends, to get away from home, or to spread the gospel. It's important to clearly understand early in the process all the motives on students' and leaders' minds.

After students have finished listing their reasons, listen together to the song "Two Weeks in Africa" by Caedmon's Call. Project or give students copies of the **Two Weeks in Africa** handout with the song lyrics. After listening to the song, debrief with these questions:

Q: **What are some of the images and themes that stood out to you in this song? How do you feel about those?**

Q: **What do you think this girl's motives were for going on this short-term mission trip? How are they similar to some of the motives we wrote for our own service? How might they be different?**

Q: **How, if at all, does this song make you think or feel differently about our justice work?**

Continue: **If nothing else, this song helps us realize we don't always have realistic expectations for what service will be like or how it will change our life or the lives of others. Stopping to think through some of these things can help us guard against a justice mission that feels like—and becomes—just a no-brainer.**

Q: **Looking at the motives we all wrote on the poster paper earlier, is there anything we've missed that we might want to consider? Are there any motives you think we might want to change?**

Q: **How do you think the people who will host us might feel about these motives?**

Q: **How do you think God feels about these motives? Are there ways we could be more God-honoring or more sensitive to the reasons God might want us to be involved in this justice work?**

Many private and public schools require some sort of "community service hours," so you may have some students participating in your event partly to meet this school requirement. If this is the case, then please ask questions like: **What is good about the motivation of "community service hours"? What might be problematic about that motivation? What can we do to overcome those potential dangers or problems?**

After you have had some good discussion about the "whys" of your trip, note to the group that asking "Why are we going?" begs a related question:

Q: **Why are we going *together*?**

Explain: **While we often focus on our personal relationships with Jesus, the Bible indicates that the ways we relate to one another are also important.**

In fact, some of the passages in the New Testament that we often interpret as applying to "me" really apply to "us." The New Testament uses a "you" that is plural—really a "you all" (or *ustedes* for any Spanish speakers out there)—to communicate some important things about the value of doing life, service, and even short-term mission trips with other believers. Let's look at a few of those Scripture passages together.

Divide students into smaller groups and have each group look up one of the two passages below. Ask them to discuss how these words of Jesus might shape the way we do justice work as a team.

1. Matthew 5:13-16

Q: **When you hear this passage, what ideas come to mind about what it means to be "salt and light" today as followers of Jesus?**

Q: **The "you" in this passage is really a "you all." How does knowing that change the way we think about what it might mean to be "salt and light"?**

Q: **Thinking specifically about our trip, how could these words of Jesus shape the ways we serve as a team?**

> In Jesus' day, salt was used to flavor foods and as a preservative, especially for meat.

2. Matthew 28:16-20

Q: **When you hear this passage, what ideas come to mind about what it means for you to "go and make disciples of all nations" today as a follower of Jesus?**

Q: **The verbs in this passage are all plural—they imply "you all" together, not just "you" individually. How does knowing that change the way we think about what it might mean to be called to "go"?**

Q: **Thinking specifically about our trip, how could these words of Jesus shape the ways we serve as a team?**

Bring the smaller groups back together to share their insights with the whole group, then move on to the final part of the discussion.

Continue: **It might be unlikely each of us would write the exact same statement about why we're going on this trip, but perhaps we can work together to create a statement expressing a common purpose and vision. A clear statement of our mission can help guard against the no-brainers that could sabotage our attitudes and our service.**

Of all the reasons we've discussed that we might use as the primary focus of our trip, what do you think is the BEST reason? Can we come up with it on one sentence?

HAVE MORE TIME?

One link that's often missing in youth short-term missions is the buy-in and full support of the church. Once your group has determined a clear purpose statement for your justice mission, you might want to take it to the church missions committee and/or senior leadership for their review, input, and support. Ideally, they would be in on the process before you get to the point of forming a student team, but we know church processes don't always work that way! The point is to take the "extra" time to be sure the wider church family is on board with what you're doing. That support will go a long way in the lives of your students and their families.

Work together with students to complete the following sentence, hopefully right there in your meeting. You might need to look at each part of this sentence separately, perhaps listing possible answers below each line, and then deciding at a later time on your final statement. Use this sentence or some variation of it to help your group create a clear purpose:

We're going to _____ **(place)**

to _____ **(what we think we're going to do there)**

because _____ **(why we feel compelled to go).**

Close by thanking God together for calling you to serve and to act with justice. You might want to use an open-ended prayer in which students can speak sentence prayers in response to your prompts, including possibly:

- prayers of thanksgiving for the opportunity to serve and bring justice;

- prayers of repentance for the ways we have served out of self-focused or harmful motives;

- prayers for God's vision and purpose to guide our group's vision and purpose;

- prayers of praise in advance for what God will do through our willingness to serve.

Johannesburg to Capetown,

the plane had barely touched down.

She was taking photos for the friends back home.

This was always where she felt her heart belonged.

And she was finally here,

the sky was bright and clear.

Two weeks...

And we all can feel the calling,

Two weeks...

to make the world a little smaller.

And so a girl got on a plane,

for two weeks in Africa.

Johannesburg to Houston,

she came home on a mountain.

But school was starting, things kept moving on.

Before you knew it, seven years had gone.

She found a picture of her,

standing, smiling,

arms around the starving kids.

She swore not to forget,

she swore not to forget...

Two weeks...

And we all can feel the calling,

Two weeks...

to make the world a little smaller.

And so a girl got on a plane,

for two weeks in Africa.

And if we follow our dear sun

to where the stars are not familiar.

Faces turn to numbers,

numbers fall like manna from the sky.

Why, oh why?

Oh Father, why?

One village in Malawi now has water running pure and clean.

One church alive in Kenya's full of truth and love and medicine.

We put the walls up,
but Jesus keeps them standing.

He doesn't need us,
but he lets us put our hands in.

So we can see,
his love is bigger than you and me.

Two weeks...

And we all can feel the calling,

Two weeks...

to make the world a little smaller.

And so a girl got on a plane,

for two weeks in Africa.

From the album *Overdressed* by Caedmon's Call. Words and music by Andrew Osenga, © 2007 House of Mirrors Music (ASCAP), admin. by Simpleville Music, Inc. Lyrics printed with permission.

MENTORING FOR JUSTICE: A STARTER GUIDE

BY BRAD GRIFFIN AND KARA POWELL

SOME SCRIPTURE

BIG IDEA: Students need a support network that includes mentors who meet with them before and after their justice work.

You'll need:

- An adult mentor or mentoring couple for each student, and a plan for helping the student and adult(s) meet.

- A copy of the **Mentoring for Justice** handout (pages 42-43) for each mentor. If you'd like, you can also make copies of the handout for students or use the similar questions in the Deep Justice Journeys Student Journal (pages 23-25).

- Optional: Consider bringing all the mentors and students together for one kickoff meeting, and provide a meal as well as a way to show the *Hitch* movie clip. If you're meeting as a whole group, be sure you have breakout space where students and mentors can talk one-on-one.

- If students are meeting with mentors outside the context of your group time, review with them your church's guidelines for appropriate adult-youth relationships (e.g., whether they should meet in a public place, whether mentors can allow students to ride in their cars).

- If your church requires background checks for potential mentors, start this process in advance.

> To find out more about mentoring, as well as ways to avoid some of the common mistakes we make in youth ministry mentoring, visit www.fulleryouthinstitute.org and search for articles using the word *mentor*.

While we all know the importance of adult relationships in kids' lives, some adults don't know what to do or say when they meet with students. Truth be told, some youth workers don't know how to coach mentors through this process. We hope this starter guide gives your adult mentors ideas to help students prepare for their justice work.

In the introductory sections of this book, we explained the important role SUPPORT plays in the experiential learning framework that shapes this curriculum. (See pages 16-20 to review this.) Adults provide essential scaffolding around students by listening well and reflecting back to students what they hear and see. We recommend that students begin meeting with mentors early in the preparation process, and that students and mentors meet several times both before and after the justice work itself. We also recommend that you think broadly as you recruit mentors; adults who might seem to be unlikely youth workers can make fantastic mentors, and good mentors come in all ages, shapes, and sizes. Involve students by asking them to suggest mentors and maybe even inviting them to find their own mentors.

For ideas on helping these mentoring relationships continue AFTER your justice work, see pages 159-161.

After you have recruited your mentors, offer copies of the **Mentoring for Justice** handout to help them get started.

To kick off your mentoring pairs, consider hosting an initial gathering for all students and mentors to help make the introduction to the process as easy as possible. If you have the capacity to do this over a community meal, that's even better. Here's a potential format for your meeting:

Bring everyone together and lead the following discussion:

Q: **What do you think of when you think of the word *mentor*?**

Q: **How would you define *mentoring*?** At some point, give this definition (or another definition you prefer) of *mentoring*: Empowering another person.

Next, play the scene from *Hitch* that is 49:30 into the movie and starts when Hitch (played by Will Smith) says, "Now about the DJ...generally I have a firm no-dancing policy." The clip ends at 52:05 when Will Smith says, "Get out," and slaps Albert Brennaman (played by Kevin James).

After playing the DVD, continue by asking the following question (making sure you draw out participation from both students and the adult mentors):

Q: **What was good about the mentoring relationship between Hitch and Albert? What was not so good?**

Explain: **Earlier I defined *mentoring* as "empowering another person," and while that's true, there's an additional clarification I'd like to make. Within the context of our faith, mentoring is not only empowering someone else, it's empowering someone *toward God's purposes.***

Q: **How can mentors help empower students toward God's purposes for them before our justice work?** If you think some of your students or mentors won't be familiar with the word *justice*, feel free to define it as righting wrongs or injustices around us.

Q: **What about *during* our justice work?**

Q: **How about *after* our justice work?**

Ask the students: **What are some of your hopes for this mentoring relationship?**

Ask the adults: **What are some of *your* hopes?**

At this point, break out into mentoring dyads or triads, letting mentors and students work through a few of the questions on the **Mentoring for Justice** handout.

When they are finished, close by coming back together for a time of worship and prayer. Make sure you thank the mentors for their investment in students, and encourage the students to do likewise.

Congratulations! You have been given the opportunity to help a student process his or her experience of serving others in seeing God's justice done on earth. Get ready for an exciting journey!

SUGGESTION 1: Do not be afraid! You might be a bit intimidated by this experience, and maybe by the person in front of you. Remember that the most important thing you can offer is your attentive presence.

SUGGESTION 2: Listen, listen, listen. Don't feel compelled to give lots of advice, and don't be scared by occasional periods of silence. Simply be a safe place for your student to speak whatever is on his or her heart.

SUGGESTION 3: You first. Remember that the person in front of you is probably scared, too. Be as transparent as possible about your own questions and fears when it comes to justice, and be prepared to share first if you ask tough questions.

SUGGESTION 4: Pray, pray, pray. Pray before, during, and after meeting with your student, and before, during, and after the justice experience. Be sure to tell your student you are praying regularly for him or her.

STARTING POINTS: The following list of ideas and questions might help you start conversations that prepare the young person you're mentoring for what lies ahead. You might pick out one or more questions to use per session, depending on how many times you will be meeting. These are simply *prompts*, not scripts, and the goal is to help your student share what he or she most needs to share.

Questions for both of you:

1. Tell me your story. What's important for me to know about who you are, where you've been, and what God is doing in your life?

2. How do other people describe you, or what do you think your friends would say about you if I asked them to describe you?

3. Read Luke 4:14-21 together. What kind of ministry was Jesus starting? Was it mostly spiritual, physical, or both at once? How does this passage describe the calling of the church today? In what ways does this Scripture passage invite us to live out justice (justice can be quickly defined as "righting wrongs")?

4. Read Micah 6:8 together. When you think of what God requires of believers, what comes to mind? Does the list in Micah seem like "enough"? Does it seem like "too much"? What are some ways you might act justly, love mercy, and walk humbly with God through this mission experience?

5. Read Luke 9:21-27 together. What do you think it means to take up your cross every day to follow Jesus? What do you think it means for you at your school or at home or at your job? What do you think it might mean during your justice work? How do you feel about being asked to make sacrifices for the sake of Christ?

Questions for the student:

1. What draws you to be part of this team/experience? What is it you're hoping for or anticipating from this justice experience?

2. What do you think life is like in the place you're visiting? How do you think it might be different from—or the same as—life here? If you were growing up there, how might you be different? How does that make you feel?

3. What do you fear about this justice mission? Where do you think those fears are coming from? What do you tend to do when you're afraid? How do you think your fears might impact your experience?

4. How do you hope to be changed by your justice work? How do you hope others will be changed?

5. As your mentor, how can I pray for you? What are three specific things I can pray for as you prepare for the justice work? What are the ways I should pray for you during the experience? How can I pray for you when you come home? How do you think I can pray for your family?

WHO'S YOUR JESUS?

BY KARA POWELL

LOTSA SCRIPTURE

BIG IDEA: When we expand our views of Jesus, we are better able to worship and serve him.

You'll need:

- The movie *Talladega Nights: The Ballad of Ricky Bobby* cued to 13:14 from the start of the movie. In this scene, Ricky Bobby, played by Will Ferrell, says grace to "the little baby Jesus." Just prior to 13:14, Ferrell refers to his "red hot smoking wife" (and uses even more coarse language than that), so make sure you've cued the DVD appropriately. We encourage you to stop the DVD at 15:30 at the line, "Let's dig in." During the two-minute scene, one of the characters says the word *damn*, so if that word is problematic in your context, either edit out that word or skip the video clip.

- DVD player

- Copies of the **Jesus-of-Choice** handout (page 46), and/or copies of the *Deep Justice Journeys Student Journal* (pages 26-28)

- Whiteboard or poster paper

- Pens

- Bread/crackers/wafers as well as grape juice (and a way to serve the bread and juice) for Communion

- A table covered with paper, with markers or crayons for students to use on that paper

- Bibles

- (HAVE MORE TIME? option: Index cards, pens, crayons)

Welcome your students and set up the video clip by explaining that Will Ferrell plays Ricky Bobby, a very successful racecar driver with...well...some interesting views about Jesus.

After the clip, lead the following discussion, writing students' responses on your whiteboard:

Q: **Why do you think Ricky Bobby likes the little baby Jesus the best?**

Q: **What other images of Jesus were mentioned in the video clip?** Some of the more humorous images are "Jesus wearing a tuxedo shirt, which says, 'I want to be formal but I'm here to party too,'" Jesus as a "Ninja fighting off evil Samurai," and "Jesus with giant eagle's wings leading an angel band."

Q: **Beyond the video clip, what pictures do people tend to have of Jesus?**

Q: **Which of the images we've mentioned have *any* sort of Scriptural validity? In other words, which pictures or images match at least a slice of the Jesus we learn about in the Bible?** Feel free to distribute Bibles if that would be helpful.

Explain: The reality is that many, maybe most, of these images have some basis in Scripture. The problem is that they represent only one little piece of him and fail to capture Jesus' full power, love, and grace.

At this point, distribute copies of the **Jesus-of-Choice** handout and walk through the various images and examples of Scriptural support.

Q: **Which "Jesus-of-Choice" do you think is most common among students today? Why do you think that is?**

Q: **Which "Jesus-of-Choice" are you most tempted to emphasize? What do you think lies behind that tendency?**

Q: **What's good about that particular image? What problems might be created by emphasizing that image and neglecting some of the others?**

Q: **Let's brainstorm together how to better encompass most of, or all, these images so we come closer to capturing all Jesus is. We don't necessarily need a single word; maybe it's a few words or even a phrase that better describes the full Jesus. What are your ideas?** Make sure to write the ideas on a whiteboard, noting which ideas seem to generate the most enthusiasm. If your students struggle with this exercise (which is likely), remind them that Jesus is beyond human words, so struggling to describe him is almost inevitable.

See if your group can agree upon an image or phrase that best describes Jesus and then ask: **How does this image relate to us as we serve? How does it relate to the folks we are serving?**

Q: **How would that image deepen our service and justice work?** If you want to help your students distinguish between service and justice, feel free to distribute the **Not-As-Deep Service vs. Deep Justice** handout on page 34.

Close by worshiping together through taking Communion, making sure you give students plenty of time to reflect upon the full Jesus and the image your team has developed as a focus. Serve the Communion elements on a table that is covered by paper, so students can write or draw the word or image that best captures the full Jesus for them. They could do this as they come to receive the elements, or after taking them. As you share the elements, you might want to say something like, "The body and blood of Jesus, who gave his *whole* life to make us whole."

HAVE MORE TIME?

Consider asking your group to think about what you could do, say, or make that might help you all stay focused on that image before, during, and after your justice work. You might even want to distribute index cards and pens or crayons so students can draw images or write words to help them reflect upon that image of Jesus in the midst of serving. Once students have finished their cards, invite volunteers to share with the entire group or divide into small groups and ask students to share their card with their small group.

At the end of the meeting, encourage students to keep these index cards in their Bibles. Or you can collect the index cards and distribute them periodically during your deep justice journey as a brief theological check-in.

JESUS-OF-CHOICE

JESUS-OF-CHOICE	SCRIPTURAL SUPPORT
Little Baby Jesus	"So they hurried off and found Mary and Joseph, and the baby, who was lying in the manger." (Luke 2:16)
Tender, Understanding Jesus	"Then neither do I condemn you," Jesus declared. (John 8:11)
Wild, Rebellious Prophet Jesus	"Jesus entered the temple courts and began driving out those who were buying and selling there." (Mark 11:15)
Great Moral Teacher Jesus	"Everyone who hears these words of mine and puts them into practice is like a wise man who built his house on the rock." (Matthew 7:24)
Santa Claus Jesus	"I have come that they may have life, and have it to the full." (John 10:10)
"Mr. Fix-It" Mechanic Jesus	"If you believe, you will receive whatever you ask for in prayer." (Matthew 21:22)
Contemplative Jesus	"But Jesus often withdrew to lonely places and prayed." (Luke 5:16)

Adapted from Chap Clark and Kara E. Powell, *Deep Justice in a Broken World* (Grand Rapids: Zondervan, 2008), 66.

FINDING MYSELF IN GOD'S STORY

BY KARA POWELL

BIG IDEA: We find our ultimate motivation for justice when we find ourselves in God's story.

You'll need:

- Four pieces of poster paper, hung next to each other
- Pens
- Bibles
- In advance: Meet with four students so they can help you explain the four movements of God's story.

LOTSA
SCRIPTURE

Welcome students and explain: **Understanding and embracing God's role in our upcoming justice work begins with understanding God's role in our lives overall. Sometimes I wonder why God would even want me—little ol' me—to be involved in God's justice work. What's helped me is to view Scripture as one big story about God's love for the world, and the pleasure God experiences as we serve in his kingdom.**

STUDENT 1: **Today, we're going to look at God's story of interacting with humans throughout Scripture. As we understand this story, we'll understand more of how God feels about us, and why and how God wants us to be involved in justice work.**

The story starts...well...in the beginning. In the first chapter of Genesis, we learn that we were created special, that we were created in God's image, which means that we were created *Good*. At this point, your first student volunteer should read Genesis 1:26-27 and write the word GOOD in large letters at the top of the first sheet of poster paper.

STUDENT 2: **Now comes the bad news. Our inherent goodness from being created in God's image has been marred by what happened in the garden of Eden. Every single person on this planet has been**

FYI: The "glory" that we have fallen short of in Romans 3:23 seems to refer to the majesty of God's holiness and...well...God's God-ness.

Adapted from Jim Hancock and Kara Powell, *Good Sex* (Grand Rapids: Zondervan, 2008)

tainted by *Guilt* because of our sin. At this point, your second student volunteer should read Romans 3:23 and Romans 6:23 and write the word GUILT in large letters at the top of the second sheet of poster paper.

Next, have your third student volunteer walk up to the third sheet of poster paper, write the word GRACE in large letters at the top, and then sit down. Give students some time to sit in silence, staring at the word. After at least 60 seconds, ask the third student to return to the front of the room and lead this discussion:

STUDENT 3: **When you think of *Grace*, what images or phrases come to mind?**

Q: **Given what we've heard about the way we are created as *Good* and then experience *Guilt* because of our sin, how should that affect the way we respond to the *Grace* God offers**?

Note: If none of your students mentions that Jesus' life, death, and resurrection are what enable us to embrace God's *Grace*, please make sure you do.

At this point, the fourth student volunteer can come up to the final piece of poster paper and write the word GRATITUDE and offer the following words:

STUDENT 4: **The *Grace* God offers us prompts us to want to serve God out of *Gratitude* for all God has done for us. Our lives become great big thank-you notes back to God.** Ideally, this student would read Ephesians 2:8-10 and then would affirm a few ways kids in your youth ministry are already living their lives as thank-you notes back to God.

At this point, help students connect the *Good/Guilt/Grace/Gratitude* story to your justice work by moving to the first piece of poster paper and asking: **How does the first part of this story that tells that we were created as Good and in God's image relate to our upcoming service?** Make sure to jot down their answers on the poster paper. (You might also encourage students to consider how the fact that *others* are likewise created in God's image affects your justice work.)

Move to the second poster paper and ask: **How does Guilt—including our own sin, the sins people have committed against us, and other sin that shapes our world—affect our justice work?**

Head to the third poster paper and ask: **In 2 Corinthians 5:17, Paul writes, "Therefore, if anyone is in Christ, the new creation has come: The old has gone, the new is here!" How does the Grace that makes us a new creation relate to our upcoming mission?**

You guessed it—stroll on over to the fourth poster paper and ask: **What would it look like to live our lives as a thank-you note back to God?**

Conclude this discussion by asking: What part of our discussion today has been especially significant for you?

Invite students to move to the poster paper that represents the element of God's story they would like to be especially mindful of in your upcoming service. Give them a few minutes to write or draw something (a few words, a picture, or a symbol) on that poster paper that reflects their thoughts and feelings about that part of God's story. Have students pray for each other in pairs or small groups, thanking God for the chance to act out this story in your upcoming justice work as well as in your daily life.

HAVE MORE TIME?

Divide students into pairs and have them practice sharing the Good/Guilt/Grace/Gratitude story with each other. After each person shares, the other should affirm what the speaker did well and offer suggestions how that person can more effectively share this divine story in the future.

WHAT DO THEY NEED MORE?

BY BRAD GRIFFIN

BIG IDEA: The gospel invites us to focus on people holistically and participate in kingdom work that serves BOTH their souls AND their bodies.

LOTSA SCRIPTURE

You'll need:

- A photograph of someone experiencing deep poverty—either from your host community or from some other part of the world. You can easily download images from organizations who serve the poor, such as World Vision or Compassion International. You only need one picture, but it helps if you have a specific name and a bit of information about the person and their context to share with the group. The point is to put a face and a name to physical needs. See the HAVE MORE TIME? idea for an alternate way to open this activity.

- Whiteboards or poster paper and markers
- Bibles
- Index cards
- Pens
- Tape
- A wall on which students can tape index cards. If that's not possible, use poster paper or a whiteboard to create a large area that will work.

Begin by asking students what some of their needs are this week—big or small. Ask how those needs are being met or going unmet, and how that is impacting their week. It might be appropriate to pause to pray for one another and lay your needs corporately before the Lord before you go on.

Next, invite students to view the photograph you've brought of the person

HAVE MORE TIME?

Have students visit a local homeless shelter, nursing home, or food pantry / soup kitchen ministry in your community. Be sure to get permission ahead of time, and send students in pairs with video cameras or voice recorders to interview caregivers they encounter. Encourage your students to ask questions about needs on various levels. Debrief the experience as part of this lesson, discussing the different ways we—and others—perceive needs. You might even use these interviews as an opener to the discussion.

Adapted from FYI's "Hungry for the Kingdom," a curriculum done in partnership with World Vision's 30 Hour Famine and available for free at www.fulleryouthinstitute.org.

49

experiencing deep poverty. If it's someone from the host community you'll visit during your upcoming justice journey, you can tailor the conversation directly around that community. If it's someone from another location, you can use this as a case study to help your group think together about holistic ministry and then apply it toward your host community and the work you hope to do there.

Describe the person and share as much as you know, then ask:

Q: **What do you think might be some of _____'s needs?**

Q: **Suppose we knew that _____ had never heard about Jesus. How many of you think _____'s biggest need is hearing about Jesus? How many of you think his/her biggest need is tangible physical support?** Depending on the situation, the needed support might be more obvious—medicine, food, education, shelter, or other needs can be mentioned here specifically.

It's inevitable that some students will say this person needs both, but don't let them choose that middle ground. Ask them to choose the one need they think is most pressing.

Divide students into two groups based on their answers and ask them to discuss the reasons for their answers.

After four or five minutes, bring the groups back together and ask them to share their ideas.

Q: **Having heard these ideas, which seem especially powerful? Do any of you want to change your mind?**

Continue: **Let's see how Jesus handled an encounter with a paralyzed man in Mark 2:1-12.** For variety's sake, you may want to ask for two volunteers to read the story—one student reads Jesus' words while the other reads everything else.

Continue: **Homes in first-century Palestine were different from most of our homes today. A typical peasant's house was a small, one-room structure with a flat roof. Some homes may have included an outside staircase that led to the roof. The roof itself was usually made of wooden beams covered with thatch and compacted earth to keep moisture from entering the house. Sometimes tiles were laid between the beams and thatch for even greater protection.**

In this passage the four men, upon seeing how crowded the one-room house was, probably carried the paralyzed man up the outside staircase, dug through the thatch and earth, and lowered him between the beams.

Q: **Does Jesus choose to help this man's soul or his body?** The answer is both.

Q: **Do you think there's any significance to the fact that Jesus forgave his sins first, before healing him? Why or why not?**

Draw a horizontal line on the whiteboard and explain: **We've been talking about two types of needs—physical and spiritual. Most people tend to think of these needs as unrelated, or as two different ends of a continuum.** At this point, write PHYSICAL NEEDS on one end of your line and SPIRITUAL NEEDS on the other end.

There's been great debate about Mark 2:5, where Mark writes, "When Jesus saw *their* faith." Does "their" refer to the faith of the four friends, or the faith of the four friends plus the paralytic's faith? The original Greek doesn't definitively say it for us. Given what you know about Scripture, what do you think?

If Jesus weren't really the Son of God, then the teachers of the law in verse 7 were right—Jesus would have been blaspheming. In Jewish teaching, even the Messiah couldn't forgive sins; only God could. The teachers weren't just being mean to Jesus; they were trying to protect their people's understanding of God.

PHYSICAL NEEDS ———————————————————————————— SPIRITUAL NEEDS

As we see from Jesus' interaction with the paralytic, the two types of needs don't lie in opposition to each other. The reality is that God's kingdom helps meet both types of needs. **Instead of a line, God's kingdom is more like a circle.** Draw a circle and write both SPIRITUAL NEEDS and PHYSICAL NEEDS inside the circle. **Both types of needs are crucial to the kingdom, and the two needs play off each other and reinforce each other.**

Q: **As we consider this image of a circle, let's think about Jesus. If Jesus were to encounter _____ and his/her family, what do you think he'd do? What do you think he'd say?** It's likely many of your students might say Jesus would try to "convert" this person by convincing them they needed eternal life. You may want to help them focus not only on Jesus' words about salvation, but also on his hopes and dreams for this person—and for others who live in despairing circumstances. Help your students think about how Jesus might want this person to experience the kingdom—not just in eternity, but also in their life and relationships here and now.

Q: **Given your previous answers, what should we be doing as we try to be kingdom followers today? What should we be saying to those who, like _____, are impacted by great need, both spiritually and physically? How is this different from what we do or say currently?**

If your students are still feeling the both-and tension in this exercise, that's okay. In fact, it's probably a good thing. Living in the midst of that tension is the key to kingdom thinking that pulls both together.

Although God's kingdom is active in the world, there's also a lot of sin in the world around us. But in the midst of sin's darkness, God's kingdom is light. Jesus himself says so in John 8:12: "I am the light of the world. Whoever follows me will never walk in darkness, but will have the light of life." And as Jesus is alive in us, we become "the light of the world" (Matthew 5:14).

Continue: **As we keep wrestling with this both-and kingdom concept, we can actually look back to the cross for a model. Jesus' death on the cross is the ultimate example of the gospel's power to meet all our needs. His death not only rescued our souls but also impacts our entire lives—including our relationships, our bodies, and our emotions.**

Now we are kingdom people who are called to follow Jesus' example. The Bible calls that *justice*— following Jesus' example of righting wrongs around us whether they be spiritual, physical, emotional, or all the above. What do you think about that explanation of justice?

Using these index cards and pens, I want you to write down the ways you see our ministry (and particularly our upcoming project) impacting people's souls or impacting the rest of their lives. Please write one item on each card. Give them a few minutes to complete this. You may want to have a few examples ready to prime the pump and you might consider giving prompts students can complete such as "Our ministry will impact souls by…" or "Our ministry will impact physical needs by…" or "Our ministry will impact relationships by…"

Continue: **Now I'm going to give you some tape. If what you've written is primarily focused on im- pacting people's souls, then I want you to tape that card to the right portion of the wall. If you think the impact is primarily on the rest of their lives—such as their bodies, emotions, or relationships—please tape that card to the left portion of the wall.** You might want to label both sides so students don't have to re- member which goes where. After students are finished, read aloud the cards on both sides.

Q: **Which items appear most frequently on the left? Which items appear most frequently on the right?**

Q: **Looking at these cards, do you think we are going to do a better job of focusing on people's souls or on their whole persons? Why do you think that is? How does that make you feel about yourself as someone who seeks to live out the kingdom?**

Q: **What connections do you see between the ways we plan to help people—both physically and spiritually—and our efforts to bring about social justice? How are our efforts to help others connected to the way we worship? How are they connected to our salvation?**

Q: **As kingdom agents, what ideas do you have for what we can and should do differently as we prepare for this justice mission?**

Q: **How can we develop a plan from these ideas so we actually *act on* them and don't just *talk about* them? Is there someone from our host community with whom we need to consult in order to best honor them in the process of trying to understand the holistic needs of the community?**

Close by gathering ideas and setting up action plans for moving toward a more holistic, justice-oriented mis- sion, and by spending time in prayer together asking God to reveal the ways he cares deeply about the bodies AND souls of the people in our host community.

BEFORE: *FRAMING* — GOD AND ME

WHERE I COME FROM

BY BRAD GRIFFIN

NO SCRIPTURE

BIG IDEA: Before we attempt to serve in another cultural context, it's important to "culturally locate" ourselves.

YOU'LL NEED:

- Whiteboard or poster paper and markers

- A blank piece of paper and a pen for each student

- Copies of the **Where I Come From** handout (page 56), and/or copies of the *Deep Justice Journeys Student Journal* (pages 35-37)

- Bibles

- Maps or aerial pictures of your community. (You can print these out ahead of time, using one of the many online mapping systems. If you know exactly who will be coming, you can print an aerial picture of each student's neighborhood. If not, simply print out multiple copies of whatever geographical boundaries will feel like "home" for your students.)

Welcome your students and have them turn to one person next to them and ask, "Where do you come from?" Give students time to ask and answer this question before continuing:

> See "Some of These Things Are Not Like the Others" on page 64 for more intentional focus on our commonality as people created in the image of God (Genesis 1:26-27).

Q: **When someone asks where you're from, what do you say?**

Q: **Do some of you have a hard time answering that question? What makes it difficult for you?** Likely there are students in your group who have moved a lot, or who were born in one place but have mostly grown up in a different state or country.

Q: **Where do our ideas about ourselves come from? Who or what tells us "who we are" and "where we're from"?**

Q: **What's behind the question, "Where do you come from"?** Give students time to share ideas, and then point out we often ask this question to help us culturally locate someone—whether that is because that person has a different accent than ours, looks different in some way, or we just want to understand them more fully by knowing where they grew up. Mention to students that when asking that question, we need to avoid making others, especially those of a different ethnicity from ours, feel uncomfortable or put on the spot.

> In many ways, culture is like the *social air we breathe*: Most of the time we don't notice it much and probably don't think about it too hard, but it deeply shapes the ways we think about ourselves, others, God, and pretty much everything else!

Continue: **Most of the time we ask about someone's roots when we encounter some way their "different-ness" from us stands out. In what ways are the people we'll be serving in our upcoming justice work most different from us? In what ways are they most similar?** Write their answers on your whiteboard.

Continue: **As we prepare to interact with folks from a culture that may be different from ours, it's a good idea to look at our own cultural location—the ways in which where we're from shapes who we are.**

Ask this question: **If you were to draw a map of your life, what might it look like? Think about the geography of your family, your beliefs, the places you've lived, the events and people significant in shaping you so far.**

Pass out copies of the **Where I Come From** handout for students to complete on their own. Then have students get in groups of three and share insights from their handouts. Get everyone back together to debrief that experience:

Q: **How did it feel to think more about your cultural location? What new insights do you have on who you are and how that shapes the way you interact with others who are different?**

Q: **How might that affect the way you love and serve others?**

Q: **What are some important things we might want to learn about the cultural location of the people we will serve during our justice work? If some of the teenagers there filled out this same list of descriptors, how do you think their lists might be similar or different from ours?** If it's not already obvious from the sharing around the room, you'll want to note that there is often quite a bit of diversity among people who live in the same location, even though an outsider might be tempted to lump everyone together based on a set of stereotypes. Just as we cannot assume we are all the same in our

HAVE MORE TIME?

Often our cultural location determines the power we have over others, or the power others have over us. It is helpful to have students think through ways their particular heritage and set of circumstances might put them in a role of power. You might ask questions like: **In what ways do we (or might we) participate in the oppression of others because of who we are and where we're from? What should we do about that?** One example might be wearing clothes made in sweatshops, where labor environments are harsh, workers are underpaid, and in some cases people are forced to work as slaves. Youth ministries have begun to speak out against such injustices, and some have begun purchasing non-sweatshop clothing or even making some of their own clothes.

youth ministry, we can't assume that getting to know one local person in our host community will mean we understand everyone.

Q: **How can we honor those we visit without being spiritual tourists who "ooh" and "ahh" over their different culture and setting?**

Q: **If the people we serve are living in poverty and we are not, how can we move beyond simply thanking God that we're not "like them"?**

At this point, distribute maps or aerial photos of your area as a prompt for the closing prayer. Invite students to pray that the Lord will help them be mindful of their own cultures, and appreciate all they have to experience by interacting with a different culture.

HAVE MORE TIME?

Have students create videos, PowerPoint presentations, posters, or culinary dishes that share about their cultural identity with the rest of the team. Give them one or two weeks to learn as much as they can about their ancestry, their family history, and their current "cultural location" and creatively share that with the rest of the group. Talk together about the ways our unique cultural heritages shape—but do not have to dictate—our interactions with others. Celebrate whatever diversity might exist among your students, and encourage one another as you continue to learn to relate to those who are different.

What makes you "YOU"? If you were a map, how would you draw you (go ahead and give it a try on the back of this handout!)? How do your history and cultural context shape the way you think, feel, and interact with others? The prompts below will give you a starting point. Try to answer each one briefly, then keep this page and return to it later as you get more thoughts and perhaps find out the answers to more questions!

- I was born in...

- I have lived in...

- I now live in...

- My family is made up of...

- My parents grew up in...

- My ancestors came from...

- I describe my race/ethnicity as...

- My house/apartment is like...

- My parents work as...

- We have _____ cars in my family.

- My family likes to eat...

- My favorite food is...

- I spend most of my time...

- When I can choose, I usually spend my free time...

- My favorite place to go is...

- The music I listen to is...

- The clothes I wear are...

- My clothes come from...

- I spend money on...

- I get money from...

Now share this list with someone else, and ask them to point out how your story shapes who you are and the unique perspective you bring to the group!

BEFORE: *FRAMING* — GOD AND US
UNITY OF THE BODY

BY TODD BRATULICH

BIG IDEA: When we are unified as a body, we are more open to the work of God's Spirit in us and more able to allow Christ to work through us as we serve others.

SOME
SCRIPTURE

You'll need:

- Intro Option A:
    - TV and DVD player or a computer with DVD drive
    - Gettysburg speech clip from the movie *Remember the Titans*. Link to it online at: http://www.flixster.com/servlet/embed/video/link/10861587 or find it in chapter 10, entitled "Lessons from the Dead," on the DVD.
- Intro Option B:
    - A large open area (indoor or outdoor)
    - Masking tape (indoors) or cones (outdoors)
    - Bicycle tire tubes (at least two for every four to six students)
- Bibles
- Poster paper or white board
- Markers
- A ball of string, twine, or yarn

INTRO OPTION A: Greet your students and set up the clip from the movie *Remember the Titans* by explaining: **Remember the Titans is a movie depicting a true story about a high-school football team in the 1960s that deals with issues of race in a newly integrated school. The tensions between the racial groups rise as the players try to claim spots on the team during training camp. This clip begins as Coach Boone (played by Denzel Washington) wakes the entire team in the middle of the night for a surprise training run.**

In John 17:21 Jesus prays that his disciples through all time will be one just as he and the Father are one. That means our goal isn't uniformity (after all, Jesus and God aren't absolutely identical) but rather a unity of purpose and mission.

Play the movie clip and then lead the following discussion:

Q: What are some of the differences that tend to divide people in your world (your school, family, community, etc.)?

Q: Why do you think it is so difficult for people to see past those differences and be unified?

Q: What are some of the differences among us on this mission team?

Q: In what ways have you noticed our differences affecting the way we interact as a group?

END OPTION A

INTRO OPTION B: Mark off a large circle with cones or tape. Have four to six students come to the center and stand inside the same bicycle tire tube with the tube at their waists, forming a circle facing outward. Explain that they are going to play tug-o-war, but in this game, it's every person for himself. The object of the game is to be the first person to get across the outside circle (cones or tape) while remaining inside the bicycle tire tube. You may need to try this out first in order to make sure your circle is wide enough and tubes are strong enough. If your tubes break, simply add another one to double the resistance and strength. After you play a few rounds, gather everyone to debrief the game.

Explain: **Sometimes in life it seems everyone is moving in his or her own direction, and it's tough to make any progress. Even as we serve together, we all have different individual goals for what we want to learn and accomplish as well as our own ways of doing things.**

Q: **Have you ever been a part of a group or a team in which it felt like everyone was doing his or her own thing? Describe your experience.**

Q: **What would happen if we all operated like this on our mission experience?**

END OPTION B

Continue: **Today we're going to talk about unity as a mission team and as the body of Christ. It might seem obvious we should be unified, but unity is often difficult to achieve, especially in an unfamiliar environment where all of us likely have our own goals and perspectives. So the first thing we need to do is ask: Why do we need unity in the midst of our justice work?** Write students' suggestions on a whiteboard or poster paper.

Continue: **Those are all great reasons to strive for unity. Jesus seemed to care a lot about unity among his disciples, as well as among those who would follow him in the future. Let's explore and find out why. In the Scripture passage we're about to read, Jesus has just told the disciples he is about to be arrested and crucified. He's praying for all his disciples—both then and now (which means he's praying for you!)** Read John 17:20-23 aloud.

Q: **Why did Jesus care that his disciples were unified?**

Q: **With whom did Jesus want the disciples to be unified?**

Q: **What other people outside of our team do you think God might want us to be unified with on this mission trip?**

Q: **What might hinder us from being unified with God, one another, or any of these other folks we have mentioned?**

Q: **What are some ways we can seek to be unified as a team this week during our service?** Write students' ideas on poster paper or a whiteboard.

Affirm students' ideas and explain that you have an activity that will help you start to feel the power of unity.

TEAM EXERCISES: (choose one or do both if you have time)

1. **Connected to the web.** Share hopes, fears, and expectations together as a group by being united by a ball of string, yarn, or twine. Begin by having a volunteer share a hope, fear, or expectation for your service. When that person finishes sharing, tell her to hold onto the end of the string and then throw the rest of the ball of string to someone else she would like to have share, ideally someone sitting across the circle. Continue this process until everyone has shared and you end up with a web of string spanning the circle. If the string is fairly strong, you can have everyone stand up and lean back a bit. At that point, share that when we are bound to one another in unity, we can hold one another up as we learn, grow, and face our fears. Then take a pair of scissors and cut the string in a few places (you may want to warn people to avoid any concussions!), which will cause the circle to collapse. Explain that when we are disconnected and left to ourselves, we may not experience all that Christ desires to do in and through us. As the string demonstrates, we are stronger together than we are on our own!

2. **Group covenant.** Write a covenant together to clarify the expectations for how your team members will treat each other. Begin with general brainstorming, making sure to create a safe environment in which every idea is heard and acknowledged. Once your students have had a chance to share their ideas, go back through the suggestions and see if your students can agree on which expectations are most important to your team's unity. Write those expectations on poster paper and invite students to sign their names at the bottom of the poster paper. Afterward, type up (or ask a student to type up) the covenant and distribute it to your team members, as well as their parents and church leaders.

Close with a prayer for unity, inviting students to repeat one phrase at a time after you:

God, we thank you for creating us
to be in relationship with one another.
We confess we often do our own thing,
seek our own interests,
and miss the blessing
of sharing in unity with one another.
Help us depend on you
and offer ourselves to one another.
Unify this team, oh Lord,
and make us a witness

to your love for the world.
Show us your heart,
your desires,
and your ways,
that we may find union
with you through your Son, Jesus Christ.
And let your Spirit work in us
and through us as we serve.
Amen.

MY GIFTS

BY KARA POWELL

SOME SCRIPTURE

BIG IDEA: We reach our full potential as the body of Christ when we work together.

You'll need:

- Copies of the **Obstacle Course** handout (page 63) or the *Deep Justice Journeys Student Journal* (pages 41-43)

- Some type of blindfolds for several students, depending on how many you assign to be "blind" during the obstacle course (see below)

Before your meeting: Make copies of the **Obstacle Course** handout, and cut along the designated lines so you have one task to give to each person.

Then create an obstacle course all of your students will go through together. Some of the students will be blindfolded and others will need to be carried, so it's wise to plan an obstacle course that is not terribly difficult. The best obstacle courses involve walking, crawling (e.g., under tables or chairs), and going up or down stairs. Whether you're meeting at your church or a home, feel free to design the course to include both an inside and outside component.

After students arrive, greet them and explain: **Today we're going to start off with a short obstacle course. The goal of the course is that everyone finishes.** It's important that you clearly explain ONCE and only once that the goal is for everyone to finish the course. Describe the actual path of the obstacle course, drawing it on the whiteboard or poster paper so students can visualize where they are supposed to go.

Continue: **I'm going to give out the tasks each of you gets to do during the obstacle course. Do not show anyone else the task I give you. You are not to act out your task until the obstacle course officially begins**. Distribute one task to each student, making sure no one else sees it. Be strategic (but subtle) in the way you give out tasks; give your most outgoing students the task of "You are mute and cannot speak at all." Give students who tend to be leaders the assignment of "You offer all sorts of suggestions, none of which is helpful, and some of which impede progress." Give students who are on the lighter side the task of "You can't move your arms or legs at all. In fact, when the game starts, just sit down."

Remind students that they shouldn't tell anyone their assignments, nor should they act them out, until the obstacle course begins. Ask students to get in a line at the start of the course. Now let the obstacle course begin!

During the obstacle course, you should traverse the route so you can note how students are doing but do NOT help anyone. Do NOT remind students of the simple goal you gave them earlier—that *everyone* finishes the course.

After your group has finished, lead the following discussion:

- **How did we do?**

- **What were some of the feelings you experienced during the course?**

- **What did I say the goal was? How did you interpret that goal?** Most students hear "everyone" and think "everyone, individually" instead of "everyone, together."

- **In what ways did you do a good job accomplishing that goal? Can you think of specific instances where people worked together to accomplish the goal?** Throughout this discussion, after students have shared their answers, feel free to add other insights or examples you noticed.

- **What are some examples of our group failing to work together to accomplish that goal?**

- **What does this activity show us about our team?**

- **What does our team do well?**

- **What areas might our team need to work on?**

Transition to Paul's teachings about the body of Christ by asking: **What Scripture passages come to mind as you think about our experience together on the obstacle course?** Chances are good that students will mention something about the body of Christ or spiritual gifts. If not, you can mention it and invite students to turn to 1 Corinthians 12:4-11.

Give a bit of history of the church in Corinth: **The church of Corinth in the first century makes our obstacle course seem like a piece of cake. As Paul learned from some members of the household of Chloe** (see 1 Corinthians 1:11), **the believers were quarreling with each other. While the church was definitely gifted** (see 1 Corinthians 1:4-8), **it was spiritually immature and full of conflict.**

Invite a volunteer to read 1 Corinthians 12:4-6, and then ask: **How would you summarize these verses in your own words? If we really believe the Spirit distributes the various gifts and talents we all have, how should that affect the way we work together?**

Read 1 Corinthians 12:7 and then ask: **What do you think Paul means by the "common good"? What does the "common good" look like for our upcoming justice work?**

Q: **Many people refer to the gifts and talents Paul is describing as "spiritual gifts." Remembering that Paul emphasizes that these gifts are for the common good, how would you define *spiritual gifts*?**

Do these lists from Paul give us an exhaustive list of the spiritual gifts? In other words, are the gifts Paul mentions in these passages the only real spiritual gifts? Paul's writings include three places where he lists spiritual gifts (1 Corinthians 12:8-11, Ephesians 4:11-13, and Romans 12:3-8). Since the lists are not identical, some scholars have suggested that, while these lists may name many (and perhaps most) spiritual gifts, they are not exhaustive. It's often proposed that other spiritual gifts exist, such as the gifts of worship and hospitality.

Invite one volunteer to read 1 Corinthians 12:8-11 and another to read Romans 12:3-8. (Depending on the time you have available, you may also want to ask a third student to read Ephesians 4:11-13.) Ask: **What are the various spiritual gifts Paul describes in these passages?** As students name the gifts, write them on the whiteboard. You might want to make sure you're familiar with your own and your church's position on prophecy, miracles, and speaking in tongues, if (or perhaps we should we say when) students have questions.

Q: **Which of these gifts do you think you, or someone else in our group, might have?**

Q: **How do you think these gifts can help us work better together as the body of Christ in our missions work?**

Q: **In these passages Paul uses the Greek word *charismata* (pronounced "care-is-MAH-tuh") to describe the gifts. The word *charismata* is derived from another Greek word, *charis* ("CARE-iss"), meaning "grace." How might thinking of your (and other people's) gifts as starting from grace affect how you view these gifts?**

Chances are good your group members will not all be aware of their own spiritual gifts, so ask: **For those of you who aren't sure what your gifts are, how can our upcoming justice work give you a better sense of what they might be?**

Read 1 Corinthians 12:11-14 and ask: **If we took this seriously, what would happen to any "gift envy" we might feel during our justice work toward others who seem to have more, or cooler, gifts than we do?**

Q: **What would the unity of our group look like?**

Close in prayer, perhaps inviting students to join hands as a reflection of the desire to work together and use their gifts more effectively in kingdom justice work.

OBSTACLE COURSE

You are mute and cannot speak at all.

You offer all sorts of suggestions,
none of which is helpful, and some of which impede progress.

Your arms and legs are stiff and you can't bend them at all.

You are blind and cannot see at all.

One of your legs doesn't work; you have to hop.
(You can switch which leg works from time to time, so you don't get too tired.)

Your arms don't work at all.

You can't move your arms or legs at all. In fact, when the game starts, just sit down.

SOME OF THESE THINGS ARE NOT LIKE THE OTHERS

BY KARA POWELL

SOME SCRIPTURE

BIG IDEA: Since the people in our group and the local people we'll be working with were all created by God, we have much in common as well as much that differs.

You'll need:

- One copy of the **Common Square** handout (page 68) for every four students, and/or copies of the *Deep Justice Journeys Student Journal* (pages 44-47)

- Whiteboard or poster paper

- Pens

- Bibles

- Index Cards

Welcome students and divide them into groups of four (if a few groups end up as threesomes, that's fine). Distribute pens and a copy of the **Common Square** handout to each group. Explain that whoever slept least last night will be Student 1, and the student sitting to that person's left will be Student 2, and around the circle to Student 3, and finally Student 4.

Explain to students that they should write things that ALL four of them have in common in the rectangle at the center of the handout. The quadrants outside the rectangle correspond to what each student has that is unique. So for instance, if all four students play soccer, they write that in the center rectangle. If only Student 2 has two sisters, that should be written in the quadrant named Student 2. If two or three students share a characteristic, it doesn't need to be written down. Students shouldn't settle for totally obvious characteristics they have in common (i.e., we're all sitting here, or we all breathe) but should try to be more creative.

Give groups five to seven minutes to come up with as many commonalities and points of distinction as possible. At the end of the exercise, have each group read all their commonalities, and then ask each student to choose ONE of their unique characteristics to share with the group.

Q: **What was easier to figure out—what you have in common or what is different among you? Why do you think that is?**

Q: **Let's think about what we know about Scripture and God's view of us. If we were to ask God what we all have in common, what would God say?** Write their answers on your whiteboard.

Affirm their answers and then explain: **The most fundamental characteristic shared by every person in this room, every person we will serve, and every other person alive, is this: Each of us was created in the image of God.** At this point have someone read Genesis 1:26-27 and then ask: **What do you think it means that God created us in his own image?**

Q: **When we are involved in service work, we can easily fall into the trap of viewing ourselves (even subconsciously) as the "great saviors" who swoop in to "rescue" others. Think about the actual people we will be interacting with in our upcoming justice work. How should the fact that every one of those people is created in the image of God affect how we interact with them?** One at a time, mention various people you'll be interacting with on your justice work, such as a local pastor, kids in the community, adults in the community, and government officials.

> Throughout history, many leaders and theologians have equated the "image of God" with some special quality or characteristic that is part of our human nature. These "substantive views" describe God's image in us as either a physical resemblance, or a spiritual quality, or even our ability to reason. More recently (in theological terms, "recently" means in the last two centuries), an important additional definition of the image of God has emerged. The "relational view" suggests the image lies not in who we are or anything we possess, but in our capacity to have relationships with God and others.

HAVE MORE TIME?

Explain: **Dr. John Perkins, cofounder and chair of the Christian Community Development Association, is an internationally known civil rights leader who has experienced racism himself as a black man in America. Dr. Perkins watched his brother die in his arms after being shot by a white police officer and was beaten himself and left for dead by his white Mississippi neighbors. Dr. Perkins is a national treasure of inspiration and insight into deep justice. In a recent interview in** *Deep Justice in a Broken World,* **Dr. Perkins commented:**

> Fundamentally, we have to understand that all people are created in God's image. That gives us all equal dignity before God. I don't see how you can accept that other humans are created in God's image with inherent dignity and then exploit them. Once we view others as created in God's image, we won't want them to live without him, and we won't want them to live in unjust social structures.[14]

Q: **Based on what you know about the people we'll be serving, how have they been exploited in the past, or how are they being exploited in the present?**

Q: **How would you feel if you experienced that exploitation?**

---

14. Clark and Powell, 93.

HAVE MORE TIME?

Q: **What are the "unjust social structures" we might encounter as we serve?** You might need to give some examples here, such as a deteriorating public education system, judicial systems that are weighted against the poor, corrupt police or government officials, lack of access to medical care, and social barriers that punish people because of their gender, ethnicity, age, or class.

Q: **Imagine that Jesus himself is one of the people you are serving, and that he is being held back somehow by these unjust social structures. (By the way, you *are* serving Jesus as you serve others in need—see Matthew 25:34-40.) What would we want to happen for Jesus? Be as specific as you can, please.** If this is a little above the heads of your students, you might try giving the following example first: Imagine that Jesus is left alone in a convalescent home, forgotten by his 12 closest friends. You'd go visit him and you'd invite some of your friends and family to go with you, too, right? You might raise money to offer special outings and opportunities for the people in the home, and you'd hire specialists to train the home operators to treat the elderly with the utmost respect and dignity. If you really wanted to change the unjust social structures, you'd also lobby your state officials to improve the health care and support systems for the elderly.

Q: **Up to now, we've talked more about what we have in common, but what are some of the characteristics that make us different from the locals we'll be serving?** Write these on your whiteboard also.

Q: **Which of these differences do you think God has allowed? Which do you think he's intentionally created?**

Explain: **The first record of significant cultural differences among humans comes in Genesis 11 in the account of the Tower of Babel.** At this point, invite students to turn and read Genesis 11:1-9.

In Revelation 7:9-12, we are given a powerful picture of God's intention that his diverse people worship him as one community. Similar descriptions of people from every nation, tribe, people, and language also occur in Revelation 5:9, 11:9, 13:7, 14:6, and 17:15.

Continue: **While many folks read this story and the resulting differences simply as a "curse," others see God's plan to create diversity in this passage. After all, God could have simply scattered people all over the earth and left them speaking the same language. Instead, God created different languages as he scattered people around the globe. Do you think there is any validity to this dual view of the Tower of Babel as a curse and a blessing? Why or why not?**

Transition to discussing your upcoming justice work by asking: What might we learn about our world and ourselves if we really love and listen to people we're serving who are somehow different from us?

Q: **What would happen if we focused only on what we have in common with the locals and not what is different?**

Q: **What if we did the opposite, focusing only on what is different and not what we have in common?**

Explain: **It's likely that at some point during this discussion, you've realized some commonalities that would be good for you to remember as we serve, as well as some distinctions. I am going to give each of you an index card and I want you to write down a few commonalities or distinctions you'd like to remember during our justice work. When you're done writing, you'll have the chance to share your thoughts with the three other people in your group.**

After a few minutes, invite students to return to their groups of four so they can share what they've written on the index cards. Ask each group to close in prayer together, praying that the Lord would help us remember both all we share in common AND the amazing diversity that God has not just allowed, but created.

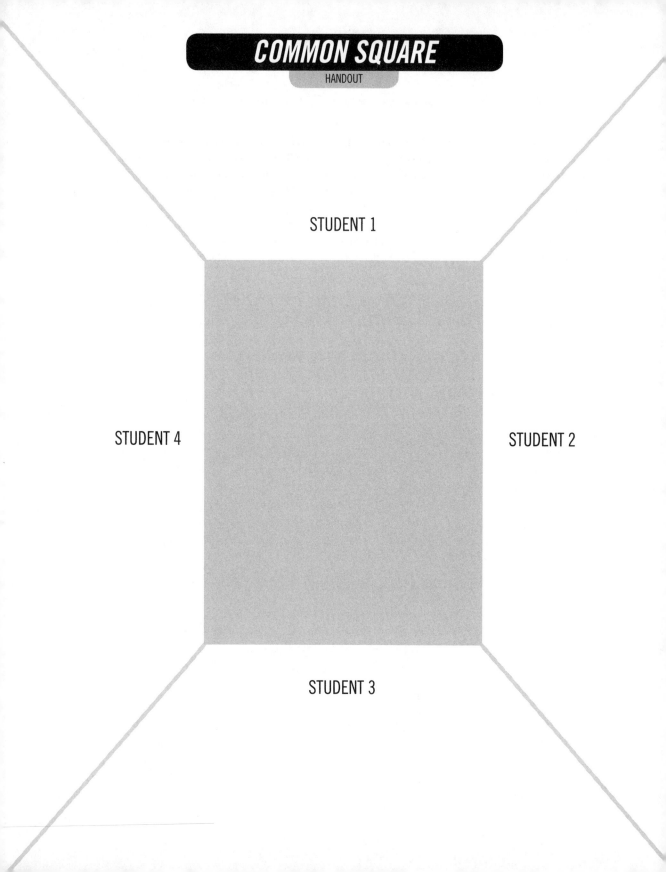

JESUS: UP CLOSE

BY DAVE LIVERMORE

BIG IDEA: God communicates his love most fully through Jesus, but get this: God also communicates his love through you and me.

SOME SCRIPTURE

You'll need:

- In your meeting space, set up three stations representing different things you'll be doing during your justice work.

  - Station 1: Food—You'll need some unfamiliar foods, preferably from the region where you're going, as well as some familiar foods your students love. In addition, have some hand sanitizer and bottled water available as well as a flip chart or poster paper with the phrase EATING LIKE JESUS written across the top.

  - Station 2: Travel—A flip chart or posterboard with the phrase JESUS-LIKE TRAVEL TIPS written across the top

  - Station 3: Work—Some black construction paper or posterboard with the phrase WORK TABOOS written across the top, and some glow-in-the-dark pens

- Pens

- Bibles

- Blank paper

Welcome your students. Explain that one of the reasons we're spending time thinking about the culture where we'll be serving is because we're trying to follow what Jesus did when he came to earth.

Q: **Imagine being God (yes, I know this is quite a stretch!). In what ways would you, as God, try to communicate who you are to the world? Be as creative as you can. Remember, you're God...** Write students' responses on the whiteboard. If students are stuck, throw out the following possibilities: God could have bellowed it from the sky, God could have put a preprogrammed chip in all of us, God could have made his message the only thing coming across television and the Internet.

Q: **What are some of the ways God reveals himself—both in the past and today? Some ways we know about from Scripture include visions, prophets, nature, a talking donkey, a pillar of fire, and, of course, Jesus.**

Ask a volunteer to read Hebrews 1:1-2. Explain: **The author writes to his or her fellow Jews a few years after Jesus' death and resurrection. The author reminds them what they know well: Their God, Yahweh, has always communicated to them in very personal ways. But now God has best revealed himself through his son, Jesus.**

> In many English translations, Hebrews 1:2 refers to Jesus as coming "in these last days." That phrase in Greek is more literally translated as "on the last of these days," a phrase indicating that Jesus' arrival on earth marked the end of one age and the beginning of a new era altogether.

Continue: **Jesus gives us an "up close" view of God and, in doing so, allows us to grow closer to God ourselves. Today, we want to spend some time practicing what it looks like to give people an "up close" view of Jesus during our justice work. The three stations we've set up represent the kinds of situations we'll encounter during our justice work.**

Divide students into three groups and have each group start at a different station. Give them three to five minutes at their first station, with the goal of thinking about what it looks like to be like Jesus in that context. After they are finished, ask the groups to rotate and repeat the brainstorming at their new station, adding to the list of ideas the previous group made. Do the same process a third time to complete the rotation. If possible, have an adult leader at each station to facilitate the exercise.

Station 1: Food

As students are trying both familiar and unfamiliar foods, ask them to eat in ways that best reflect Jesus in the midst of new (and maybe yucky-tasting) experiences. Ask students to discuss what it will mean to the locals we're serving if we eat their food, as well as the messages communicated if we don't (or if we hold our noses and groan as we do). Similarly, distribute hand sanitizer and bottled water and have students practice how to use both inconspicuously.

Station 2: Travel

How will our behavior while traveling to our destination and while traveling from place to place reflect Jesus? Students might need to be prompted to think about things like volume level, how we interact with strangers, and when and how to take pictures.

Station 3: Work

How can the work we do give others (and ourselves) accurate pictures of what Jesus is like? Topics to discuss here include laziness or being too focused on tasks, excluding the locals from joining us, and complaining.

When the three groups have finished all three stations, spend some time as a large group debriefing the exercise.

Q: **In which of these areas will it be most challenging for you person-ally to live out Jesus' incarnation? Which will be easiest?**

Q: **How can we help one another live more like Jesus throughout our upcoming justice experience?**

Close in prayer by walking with your students to each of the three stations and spending a minute or two at each, together asking that people would get an "up close" view of Jesus in the way we love and serve the locals (as well as one another).

HAVE MORE TIME?

Give your students a chance to think about how the local people are likewise reflecting Jesus in their food, travel, or work.

LOCAL MOTION

BY KARA POWELL

NO SCRIPTURE

BIG IDEA: True partnership means understanding the ministry strategy of the people in our host community.

You'll need:

- TV or video projector

- DVD or VCR player

- A DVD or videotape featuring clips from a few TV shows that are popular with your students. You can create your own tape the week before the meeting by recording clips from a handful of different shows. If possible, you should choose TV shows that some students follow closely while other students couldn't care less. Your goal is to find clips that wouldn't make sense if you hadn't been following previous episodes or even earlier parts of the show (so lean toward serials like *Heroes* and *Lost*). If you'd like, you can show movie clips instead of TV clips.

- Ahead of time, figure out a way you can ask (by e-mail, phone, or letter) some of the local leaders in the community you'll be serving the questions your students will suggest during this meeting.

- Whiteboard or poster paper

- Pens

Welcome students and explain that you have some TV clips to show them. Play about 30 seconds of your first clip and then ask: **How many of you watch this TV show? How many of you don't? For those of you who don't, what do you think is going to happen during the rest of this episode?** Let a few students who don't watch the show guess what's going to happen, and then let students who watch the show explain what really happens. Continue this exercise for your remaining TV clips.

Then lead the following discussion:

Q: **What did those of you who watch the various shows know that the rest of us didn't?**

Explain: **I don't know about you, but I really hate it when I miss the first few minutes of a movie. I feel behind and wonder if I'm going to be able to really understand the rest of the movie. It's awfully hard to jump into the middle of a story. In what ways is our upcoming justice work similar to jumping into the middle of a story?**

Q: **What disadvantages might the locals experience since we are jumping into the middle of their story?**

Q: **God is constantly at work, all over the world. What disadvantages will we experience as a group since we are jumping into the middle of what God is already doing among the locals?**

Q: **What advantages, if any, might there be to us showing up without knowing the full story of the local people?**

Q: **What questions would you want to ask the locals about their story?** Write down their suggestions on the whiteboard.

Q: **What questions would you want to ask about how God is at work in their ministry? What questions do you have about their ministry strategy?** Similarly, write down their suggestions on the whiteboard.

Q: **How might asking these questions and gaining answers deepen our service and justice work? How might they deepen our relationships with the locals?**

Explain your plan for asking these questions (by e-mail, phone, or letter) of some of the local leaders. If it's possible to set up a way to talk to some of the local leaders by phone (or some other way) right then and there, that would be ideal. If not, make a commitment to report the answers back to your students at a future meeting.

Even better, consider bringing a leader from the host community to talk with your group. This is likely a big investment, but it might be worth it—both for students and for the host community. If it seems appropriate, invite a few students to take responsibility for asking the questions, or to share that responsibility with you.

GIVE AND RECEIVE

BY KARA POWELL

LOTSA SCRIPTURE

BIG IDEA: We have much to receive from—and give to—those who have less material "stuff" than we have.

You'll need:

- The video *Teenage Affluenza*, available through World Vision at http://www.30hourfamine.org/portal/pages/leader/fuller.html

- Computer and projector or some other way to show the video

- Whiteboard or poster paper

- Pens

- Bibles

This exercise assumes your students do not perceive themselves as "poor." If that is not the case, then please rephrase your questions and comments to reflect the awareness that some of your own students face poverty themselves.

Explain: **Today we're going to watch a video about a disease you might have—and not even know it.** You might want to explain that the video you're showing was actually made in Australia, so there are a few differences (e.g., they drive on the other side of the road). Play the video and then ask:

Q: **How would you define *affluenza*?** You might want to point out that the term *affluenza* came from combining the words *affluence* (another word for wealth) and *influenza* (another word for the flu).

Q: **What are its symptoms?**

Adapted from FYI's "Hungry for the Kingdom", a curriculum done in partnership with World Vision's 30 Hour Famine and available for free at www.fulleryouthinstitute.org.

HAVE MORE TIME?

Q: **Let's think about the differences between teenagers with affluenza like Erin and teenagers in the rest of the world whom we saw in the video.** Get ready to write down the differences in two columns on your whiteboard with one column labeled "TEENS WITH AFFLUENZA" and the other column labeled "TEENS IN DEVELOPING NATIONS." **What are the differences in...**

- **The way they get to school?**
- **What they do during the day?**
- **Their chores?**
- **Their food?**
- **Their safety?**
- **The things they own?**

Q: **Let's think even beyond what we saw in the video.** At this point you might consider dividing your group into two, with one half speaking up for "teens with affluenza" and the rest of the group speaking up for either "the rest of the world" or "teens in the place we're serving." (You can choose which makes the most sense for your ministry.) Continue to write both groups' answers on the whiteboard as you discuss the following questions:

- **What brings you the most joy?**
- **What causes you the most stress?**
- **What aspects of God's character are especially meaningful to you?**
- **If you were to travel and visit someone from the other group and see that person's lifestyle, what would be your first impressions?**
- **What would you envy in the other person's life?**
- **For what in your own life would you feel grateful?**
- **If someone gave you $1,000, how would you spend it?**

Q: **Chances are good many of us—maybe even all of us—in this room, suffer from at least a mild case of affluenza. As we think about the kids we're going to interact with in our upcoming justice work, what might we learn from kids who don't have as much affluenza as us?** Note: Many youth workers ask this kind of question on mission trips, and students tend to respond, "They're so happy, even though they have a tough life." Try to help students move beyond that typical "they're so happy" answer to some deeper lessons we could learn from them.

Q: **What do you think our upcoming project might teach us about relationships with others?**

Q: **What do you think we might learn about God and God's kingdom?**

For more on how to talk with your kids about the misconception that "they're so happy," see "If You're Happy and You Know It…Smile" on page 107.

At the time Jesus gave his Sermon on the Mount, he couldn't escape the growing crowds (see Matthew 4:23-25). And his teachings in Matthew 5—7 likely occurred over a period of a few days, not a few hours. In Matthew 5:1 we're told Jesus "sat down" to teach. It was customary for synagogue leaders and schoolteachers to stand while reading Scripture, but to sit while teaching.

At this point, ask students to turn to Matthew 5:3-10. Explain: **These verses in Matthew, known as the Beatitudes, kick off Jesus' Sermon on the Mount, a message he gave before a large crowd near the Sea of Galilee. We're going to read the verses one at a time. After every verse, I want us to discuss two questions:**

1. *How might these verses be relevant to kids suffering from affluenza?*

2. *How are they relevant to kids who are affluenza-free?*

Read the verses one at a time, integrating some of or all the following insights as appropriate:

- Matthew 5:3 uses the phrase "poor in spirit" while the parallel passage in Luke 6:20 just says "poor."

- The reference in Matthew 5:4 to "those who mourn" probably relates not only to people who mourn the loss of someone who has died but also to those experiencing grief over sin.

- "Meek" in Matthew 5:5 doesn't mean being a doormat others walk all over. Instead, it means being gentle and showing self-control.

- The phrase "hunger and thirst" in Matthew 5:6 expresses a person's deep desire.

- "Righteousness" probably means both our individual "right living" before God, as well as justice in our communities and world.

- "Mercy" in Matthew 5:7 embraces both the forgiveness of others, and compassion for the needy who are suffering.

- "Pure in heart" in Matthew 5:8 means both inner moral purity and single-mindedness.

- Jesus is the ultimate peacemaker, bringing peace between God and the human race, as well as among humans. In Matthew 5:9 Jesus promises that those who follow his example in peacemaking will be heirs of the kingdom ("children of God").

- As Jesus' life illustrates, being peacemakers will often (maybe always!) cause others to oppose (or persecute) us, as we read about in Matthew 5:10.

Q: **Let's look at Matthew 5:11-12 together. What kind of heavenly reward awaits those who are persecuted? What do you think Jesus means?**

Continue: **When we get involved in a service project—especially one that takes us to a nation or community poorer than our own—we may think of ourselves as the "givers" and the people there as the "receivers." And it's true that many Americans have far greater financial resources than people in other parts of the world—and those resources can and should be shared to help those in need. Yet one-sided relationships—in which one side always "gives" and the other side always "receives"—rob both sides of**

dignity. As we've just seen, people who have far less money than we do can often give us great insight into kingdom truths about life and God that we might otherwise miss.

Q: **In addition to learning from them, what are other ways we can "receive" from them?** Ideas include letting them prepare food for you, being grateful if they give you a gift (even something very small), and inviting them to lead portions of worship gatherings you have as a team.

Close by inviting your students to pray aloud as they feel led, encouraging them to sit with their arms in an open position as if they were actually receiving a gift, as a reminder of all we have to learn and receive from those with whom we partner.

CRISSCROSS CULTURE

BY DAVE LIVERMORE

SOME SCRIPTURE

BIG IDEA: Our culture shapes what we view as "normal" and how we view the world.

You'll need:

- Copies of the Info Form handout (page 81), and/or copies of the *Deep Justice Journeys Student Journal* (pages 54-57)

- A few 3x5 white index cards with green magic marker lines drawn on each of them in random patterns (go crazy, you creative types)

- Whiteboard or poster paper

- Pens

- Bibles

- Information about the culture/people you'll be visiting (from Web sites, books, magazines, or laptops with Internet access)

Welcome your students and distribute the **Info Form** handout to them, asking them to follow your instructions very carefully. Give the green and white cards to a select few. Read the following instructions:

1. **Write from right to left.**
2. **Write as clearly as possible.**
3. **Fill in every blank.**
4. **Do not fill in #8 unless you received a green and white card.**
5. **You have four minutes to complete this.**
6. **You can't ask any questions.**

Repeat the instructions one time and then have them begin.

After you've given them four minutes, lead the following discussion, writing students' responses on the whiteboard:

Q: **How did you feel as you filled out this form?**

Q: **What frustrated you about this form?** If students talk about it being "wrong" or "backward," challenge their assumptions about why writing from left to right is the "right" direction. (Point out that more than half the Bible was originally written in Hebrew, which is read from right to left.)

For more on the importance of "culture," see "Where I Come From" on page 53.

Q: **For those of you who didn't receive index cards, how did it feel? What about for those of you who did receive the cards?** Feel free to talk about how "random" opportunities are given, and how that creates instant advantages (or in some cases, disadvantages).

Q: **What confused you about this form?** Feel free to explain that the options for "Grade in School" are based upon the system many countries use (Primary 5 and 6, Secondary 1-4, and Junior College 1 and 2).

Q: **How did it feel to be given options that don't fit what you're used to?**

Q: **How did you feel about the language choices?**

Explain: **Understanding the way culture shapes how we and other people see the world is an important part of our justice experience. Missionaries and justice workers have been talking about the importance of adapting to culture for two thousand years. Let's look closely at how one of Scripture's best-known leaders approached culture.**

On the back of the Info Form, I'd like you to write down the cultural groups Paul "became like" in 1 Corinthians 9:19-23. At this point, invite a volunteer to read the passage out loud as the rest of the group writes down the various groups with whom Paul interacted.

In 1 Corinthians 9, Paul refers to two types of law: The "law" in general (sometimes called "God's law"), which refers to the Old Testament law and practices, as well as "Christ's law," likely meaning Christ's teachings and their implications.

Q: **Some people claim that this passage means it's okay to become a chameleon, going with the flow of whatever the people around you are doing. How would you respond to that?**

Q: **If we could ask Paul when it's okay to adapt to the culture of others and when it's not okay, what do you think he would say?**

HAVE MORE TIME?

Q: Before Paul became a follower of Jesus, he was a powerful and prestigious ruler. He was obeyed and envied. Note how Paul describes himself in 1 Corinthians 9:19. How would you have felt if you went from royalty to becoming a slave?

Continue: Paul's not the only leader in Scripture who went from royalty to slavery. That's exactly what Jesus did, too. Jesus went from being fully God to also embracing human culture. How do you think that felt?

Q: What aspects of human culture might have been pleasant for Jesus, who was and is, you know... God?

Q: What parts of human culture would have been unpleasant for Jesus?

Q: Let's apply this to our own upcoming justice work. What do you already know about the culture in which we'll be serving?

Continue: Let's divide into groups of two or three and spend 10 or 15 minutes finding out as much as possible about the culture we'll be encountering. Distribute books, magazines, and travel information, as well as laptops with Internet access if possible.

When groups are finished, ask each group to report on the three or four most interesting insights they discovered about the culture where you're headed.

Refer back to the frustration students may have felt in filling out the **Info Form** and then ask: **In light of what we just learned about the culture where we're heading, what things might be frustrating for us there?**

Q: If we want to learn to appreciate cultural differences rather than see them as wrong or abnormal, what should we do?

Q: In what ways might our own culture seem awkward or frustrating to others?

Conclude by reminding students we don't have to wait for our service experience to notice different cultures and the way culture shapes people's behavior. Encourage your students to become more aware during the next week of the different cultures around them, such as different ethnic groups or different groupings at school (like the athletes or the indie music crowd or the techies).

As you close in prayer, invite students to write down the name of one student at school who has a different culture. Together with your students, ask God to allow us to become all things to this student we'll encounter this week—as well as to those we'll be interacting with during our upcoming justice work—for the sake of the gospel.

_____ EMAN .1

_____ EGA .2

_____ ELAM _____ ELAMEF :REDNEG .3

_____ HTRIB FO YTIC .4

LOOHCS NI EDARG .5

____2J ___1J ____4S ____3S ____2S ___1S____ 6P ____ 5P

_____ PIRT SIHT NO OG OT TNAW UOY NOSAER .6

_____

_____ CIBARA _____ NAMREG _____ IAHT :NEKOPS SEGAUGNAL .7

_____ REHTO

_____ YTIVITCA ETIROVAF .8

YOU SAID *WHAT?*

BY DAVE LIVERMORE

SOME SCRIPTURE

BIG IDEA: The way we talk about our justice work reveals something about our assumptions and our hearts.

You'll need:

- Copies of the **Reaching Consensus** handout (page 84) and/or copies of the *Deep Justice Journeys Student Journal* (pages 58-61)

- Pens

- Bibles

Welcome your group and tell them you're going to think together about how you talk about your team and your shared mission together.

Q: **Think about a time someone said something that really shocked you. Who was it and what did he or she say?** You may want to encourage students to keep their shocking examples PG-13 or you might be hearing from some parents in the morning.

Give a few students a chance to share examples. Some might have been good things, others not so good.

Q: **What connection if any is there between our words and our hearts?**

Invite volunteers to look up the following Scripture passages and read them: Proverbs 13:3; 17:27; 18:4; Ephesians 4:29; James 3:3-6.

Q: **What stands out from these verses?**

Q: **Proverbs 18:4 has some interesting imagery about deep waters and a rushing stream. What do you think that means?**

Q: **James 3:3-6 compares the tongue to a ship's rudder—the small blade at the back of a boat that controls its direction. Why do you think James likens the tongue to such a small but important part of the ship?**

Q: **Why do you think James believes the tongue has the power to corrupt the "whole person"?**

Continue: **There are really obvious things we should avoid in our speech, like lying, gossip, and**

profanity. But sometimes the subtle things that get said are equally dangerous because of what they communicate.

Teams doing justice work are often asked to share about their experiences before they go and after they return. The ways we talk about those experiences are really important.

Distribute copies of the **Reaching Consensus** handout (page 84). Explain that these are comments often made by short-term mission participants. Have each student write whether they agree or disagree with the statement. Tell them not to "over-think" their responses. Just write down the first response that comes to mind. They must choose one or the other—Agree or Disagree.

NOTE: There are two copies of the **Reaching Consensus** handout: One for you to give students and one marked **Reaching Consensus Leader's Handout** to aid you in debriefing the exercise.

After students are finished, divide them into groups of four or five and have them compare their responses.

Ask each group to choose one statement for which they didn't all put the same response. The group should rewrite the statement so they can all agree with it. The statement they write should still pertain to the original idea that was written.

If time allows, they can do this again with a second statement.

NOTE: The goal is not so much to focus on whether students come up with the "right answers" as it is to have them identify problems in the statements and move toward a better way of expressing the statement.

Have the groups report back and share the statement they rewrote and why. Debrief all the statements with your students, using the **Reaching Consensus Leader's Handout** as a springboard for conversation.

Q: **How might the ways we talk about our justice work shape how we actually do it?**

Close in prayer, asking the Lord to help all of you think carefully about how you talk about your upcoming justice mission with one another and to others. The ways you talk about it will shape how you actually do it!

"A" for Agree
"D" for Disagree

It's hard to work with people who don't speak English.

Mexicans do many things backward from how we do them.

Many of the problems of people in Africa are related to their lack of initiative.

Everyone should learn English because it's the language of opportunity in the globalized world.

Americans are very generous.

Poor countries usually have corrupt governments.

The people here are dirt poor. We're so blessed to born in America.

Most Americans have too much stuff.

We're bringing the gospel to Guatemala.

Notes for your consideration as you teach this lesson:
Whether students put "Agree" or "Disagree" really isn't the point. It's more to see the assumptions behind the statement.

It's hard to work with people who don't speak English.

* Why emphasize that the people you are working with don't speak English instead of that we don't speak Spanish or Portuguese? It's a subtle way of thinking about your role.

Mexicans do many things backward from how we do them.

* "Backward" implies negative or not as smart. Simply talking about it as "different" would be more helpful.

Many of the problems of people in Africa are related to their lack of initiative.

* That could be partly true, but there are also systemic forms of injustice that hinder people (e.g., lack of access to education, biased criminal systems, historic forms of classism).

Everyone should learn English because it's the language of opportunity in the globalized world.

* English is one language of opportunity—but not the only one. And "should" is a bit strong.

Americans are very generous.

* While some Americans are extremely generous, there is no evidence that Americans tend to be more generous than persons from other nations. And the U.S. government gives substantially less than other developed nations.

Poor countries usually have corrupt governments.

* This may be true. It could be helpful, however, to point out that we aren't short on corruption in our own government.

The people here are dirt poor. We're so blessed to born in America.

* While attention to poverty is important, overemphasis on words like "dirt poor" sound arrogant. And if we assume Americans are "blessed," does that imply that people born outside the United States are not blessed—or even "cursed"? Lots of people from other parts of the world consider it a blessing to be Mexican, Kenyan, or Chinese. (By the way, people living in Central and South America also see themselves as living in "America.")

Americans have too much stuff.

* While only 5 percent of the world's population lives in the United States, our country consumes 50 percent of the world's resources. We are a very rich nation. Yet it's also important to remember there are people in the United States living in extreme poverty, too!

We're bringing the gospel to Guatemala.

* The gospel is present through the Holy Spirit and the Christian church in every country in the world. We're joining what God is already doing wherever we go.

A FRIENDLY HEADS-UP TO YOUTH WORKERS!

One of the learning exercises we suggest you might use AFTER your justice work (page 151) will work *way* better if you do a bit of setup BEFORE your work begins. Plus, it's always a good idea to facilitate students praying for each other.

So consider trying the following:

Before your mission begins (ideally early in your preparation process), pass index cards out to your students and ask each of them to write their name at the top of the card, and then to list two personal prayer requests for this justice work. Be sure to let them know before they start writing that these requests will be shared with other students, not just with adults, and that they will be praying for one another using these cards.

Then gather the cards and redistribute them to students, either randomly or intentionally (just be sure no one ends up with his or her own card!) Instruct each student to pray for the person whose card they receive throughout your team's preparation and during your justice mission. Invite students to keep these cards by their beds or in their Bibles—wherever they will see the card frequently and be reminded to pray. If you'd like, you can either ask them to keep their prayer partners a secret or to encourage each other by letting individuals know they are receiving prayer.

DURING:
EXPERIENCE & REFLECTION

Helping your students—and yourself—
pause once or twice each day to pay
attention to the deep insights
in your justice journey.

KEEP IT SIMPLE...

BY BRAD GRIFFIN AND KARA POWELL

DEVOTION
friendly

NO
SCRIPTURE

BIG IDEA: Ongoing reflection on a few simple questions can give your trip a sense of cohesion and your students a sense of God's ongoing transformation.

You'll need:

*   Copies of the **Ten Simple Reflection Questions** handout (page 89), and/or copies of the *Deep Justice Journeys Student Journal* (pages 64-65)

This book is designed to give your team members all sorts of creative ways to interact with one another as you discover what God is showing you during your justice journey. But the reality is that sometimes it's better to keep it simple. If your group is running low on either energy or time, feel free to choose a few items from the **Ten Simple Reflection Questions** handout as a simple but effective tool to process all you're experiencing as individuals and as a group.

The youth ministries that tested this curriculum during its development found that choosing a few questions and asking them regularly throughout their justice journey gave students helpful reflection anchors and also gave their trip a sense of cohesion. You could also accomplish those goals by periodically repeating with your team the "Prayer of Review" exercise on pages 90-92.

TEN SIMPLE REFLECTION QUESTIONS

1. What was most life-giving for you today?

2. What was most draining or life-depleting today?

3. Where did you see or experience growth today?

4. How did you experience Christ today?

5. Where did you see God at work today?

6. When did you feel overwhelmed, frustrated, or undone today?

7. What person or experience was most significant for you today and why?

8. How are you being stretched?

9. What are you most thankful for right now?

10. On a scale of 1 to 5, what overall rating would you give to today? Why?

PRAYER OF REVIEW

BY KURT RIETEMA

DEVOTION
friendly

NO
SCRIPTURE

BIG IDEA: God is constantly present with us. From time to time we can stop and prayerfully review God's presence in our lives and even the way he shows himself through others.

You'll need:

- Just this prayer

As a leader you may find it difficult to know how long to pause in silence after each question or prayer prompt. The silence may seem awkward at first, but giving enough time between questions gives enough space for you and your students to think and recall the day. To help, we've provided you with a suggested guide for counting after each question or prayer prompt. If you'd like, you or someone else can gently strum a guitar in the background to help focus your students' hearts and minds as bookends to the prayer, but silence is preferable for the prayer itself.

In the midst of your justice work, many factors work against fruitful reflection times—the schedule itself, cross-cultural adjustment, and even group dynamics prevent us from moving with students into deeper and more insightful reflection. This prayer exercise is adapted from a Prayer of Review that has been faithfully practiced by Christians of the Jesuit tradition for centuries. It is intended to help slow down your students' minds (and your own mind) so you can sift through the noise of the day's experiences and become more aware of the ways God has been present to you, perhaps even through others.

Begin by asking: **Would a few of you be willing to share brief descriptions of what you personally experienced today?**

Continue: **For most of us, today was probably a sprint through a host of unfamiliar and unknown experiences. In order to help us sift through the noise of the day's experiences and become more aware of how Christ has been present to us, we're going to walk together through a Prayer of Review. We will begin by recalling people, places, and events. As we do, I want us to take note of our feelings. For the next several minutes, I would like for us to slow down, close our eyes, and focus on the small or large ways in which God has been present to us. Let's begin our prayer together.**

This Prayer of Review was adapted from www.pray-as-you-go.org, a website of Jesuit Media Initiatives.

Take a moment now to stop, to become still and focused. *(Count to 6 slowly.)*

Let your breathing help you relax as you breathe in and out. *(Count to 10 slowly.)*

As you begin the prayer, ask God to guide your thoughts, feelings, and reactions so you might see God's presence in your life. *(Count to 10 slowly.)*

And now begin to recall the day:

How did you feel when you woke up this morning and during the first part of the day? *(Pause.)*

What was happening? *(Pause.)*

What sort of mood(s) were you in? *(Count to 10 slowly.)*

How did you spend your morning and the middle of the day? *(Count to 3 slowly.)*

Where were you? *(Pause.)*

Whom were you with? *(Pause.)*

What was happening? *(Count to 10 slowly.)*

Now let your memory drift over your afternoon and evening, recalling events, people, and places. *(Count to 12 slowly.)*

With whom did you most connect? *(Count to 6 slowly.)*

Why do you think that was? *(Count to 6 slowly.)*

How were you feeling at different times? Try to name for yourself the different moods you felt. *(Count to 8 slowly.)*

As you consider your whole day, when did you notice times of light or life? *(Count to 6 slowly.)*

What gifts have you received today? *(Count to 6 slowly.)*

Take a moment to relish these and give thanks to God for them. *(Count to 15 slowly.)*

If there have been difficult times or difficult people, notice them, too, offering them to God that he may send his grace and love into them. *(Count to 10 slowly.)*

So where have you known the God of life today? *(Pause.)*

Where have you seen the face of Christ in others? *(Count to 10 slowly.)*

Take a moment to talk to God as you would a friend about your day. *(Count to 15 slowly.)*

As this day comes toward its end and you look forward to the next, is there anything you want to ask of God for the coming day(s)? Take a moment to do this before you bring your prayer to a close. *(Count to 60 slowly.)*

After the prayer is finished, you have a couple of options. First, you could give students some time alone to journal about how God has been present to them and how they've seen Christ in others. Perhaps students could use that time alone to write a note to a person who has been Christ to them or to seek reconciliation with those with whom they've been in conflict.

A second option is to invite students to share aloud ways they've seen Christ through others in the group, so everyone can be encouraged. If you choose the second option, prep your adult leaders ahead of time to make an effort to share how they've seen Christ through students who don't get mentioned by other students. If you choose this second option, consider using the following discussion guide:

As we come back together, let's take some time to share what God revealed to us during the Prayer of Review and how God has been present to each one of us.

Q: **What things did God reveal to you during the prayer?**

Q: **What unexpected gifts did you receive today?**

Q: **If you feel comfortable sharing about them, what times of difficulty or darkness did you feel today?**

Q: **Where did you see the face of Christ today in others, either locals or your team members?**

Q: **What are you asking of God for the coming day(s)?**

Close by giving students a few minutes to pray silently. Invite them to pray individually or to join with another student for a brief prayer. If they have time, they can move on and pray with another student. The goal is to give students freedom to pray individually or to pray with others, perhaps even others who have somehow embodied Christ in the midst of your justice work.

CAN YOU HEAR ME NOW?

BY DAVE LIVERMORE

BIG IDEA: We have the huge privilege of building relationships with the locals by listening.

You'll need:

- Copies of the **We Said; They Said** handout (page 95), and/or copies of the *Deep Justice Journeys Student Journal* (pages 68-70). If being on location makes carrying or copying these materials difficult, just ask a few students to read the quotations aloud.

- Bibles

- Pens

- Paper

Greet your group and ask: **As we were involved in justice work today, what did we hear from the people we served?**

Explain: **Some researchers who study short-term missions suggest that, without realizing it, service teams like ours can miss one of the greatest opportunities of being on a mission like this—encountering and listening to the people who live here!**

One of those researchers, Dr. Terry Linhart, went with a youth group to Ecuador. He described the students' experience as being like people who go to a museum. At the museum, we look at artifacts from another time through glass but it's hard to really immerse ourselves in what that time period was like. Even though the youth group Dr. Linhart was with loved, served, and worshipped alongside Ecuadorians, they were never really able to move their interactions past smiles, regular utterings of "*gracias*," and some hugs.[15]

Q: **How does our experience so far compare with that other youth group's experience?**

---

15. Terence Linhart, "They Were So Alive: The spectacle self and youth group short-term mission trips" (paper presented at the North Central Evangelical Missiological Society Meeting, Deerfield, IL, April 9, 2005), 7.

Q: **In what ways does it feel like we're viewing people through a display case in a museum?**

During this discussion, push your students beyond quick, easy responses. Wrestle together with whether we can honestly say we're interacting with the local people. Do we know their names? Do we know their backgrounds? Their stories? What have we *really* learned about them?

Distribute the **We Said; They Said** handout and read through it together. After each pair of sayings, discuss the problems evident in the perspectives of the North Americans.

Q: **What quotations on this handout might feel similar to things we are thinking or saying as we serve?**

Q: **How are we acting or talking differently?**

HAVE MORE TIME?

Invite your students to rewrite Proverbs 12:15 (either individually or in groups) as a prayer expressing a commitment to listening to the locals you're with during your justice work. After students have finished writing their prayers of commitment, go around and read them aloud in prayer.

Q: **What kinds of things can we do to avoid seeming like the people in the quotations on *We Said; They Said*?**

Q: **In many cultures people would be too embarrassed to tell us explicitly if we're being offensive. So we have to watch for cues. As we interact with the locals here, what clues would tell us we are being sensitive and honoring to them? What clues might tell us we're not?**

Invite a volunteer to read Proverbs 12:15.

Q: **What would the "way of fools" look like for us while we're here?**

Q: **What kind of advice can the locals here offer us, not just about any tasks we're trying to do, but also in light of what they observe in U.S. culture?**

Continue: **The reality is that we can't all get to know every single person here really well. So let's each think of one or two local folks (not teammates) we've met whom we'd really like to get to know better in the midst of our justice work. What can we do tomorrow to get to know those people better? How specifically can we begin to practice listening well to them?**

Invite students to get into pairs, perhaps even encouraging them to pair up with teammates they don't know all that well. Ask students to share with each other the names of the local persons they'd like to get to know better, and then have them pray together that God would strengthen those relationships in the days to come. When the pairs have finished praying, ask students to touch base with their prayer partners tomorrow at lunch as a type of accountability for their goal of getting to know a local better. At lunch, they can ask their partners if they've had a chance to spend time with that local and identify any other ways they can build a deeper relationship with that local during the rest of the day.

You might want to offer two suggestions to your group members as they pursue deeper connections with the people you're serving. First, caution them against pursuing deeper male/female relationships since the lines of appropriate relationships can get blurry, especially when different cultures are involved. Second, discourage your students from making promises to stay in touch unless they're really going to do it.

North Americans...

"We've got to do something. The window of opportunity is NOW! The time for change is ripe. We must seize this opportunity."

A recurring statement made by short-term missions (STM) teams

Locals...

"You too quickly get into the action without thinking through the implications for our churches long after you go home."

A recurring concern voiced by local believers who receive STM teams

North Americans...

"They're dirt poor. It just makes me realize how blessed I am to be born in America."

One of the most common statements made by STM teams. It's usually combined with a statement about the happiness of the poor people encountered.

Locals...

"I can still feel like a stranger in the American Church, especially when short-termers return from India bubbling over their accomplishments and describing my birthplace as a land of deprivation."

A comment from an Indian-American woman on the ways STM teams obsess over the poverty of places visited

North Americans...

"It felt really good to work so hard. We gave them some buildings they never would have had without us being there."

A recurring statement made by STM teams

Locals...

"I found out soon enough that I was in the way. The group wanted to do things their way and made me feel like I didn't know what I was doing. I only helped the first day."

A comment from an Honduran bricklayer who planned to help a team build houses for hurricane victims

Adapted from Dave Livermore's *Serving with Eyes Wide Open* (Grand Rapids: Baker Books, 2006).

SHARING OUR STORIES

BY KARA POWELL

DEVOTION friendly

SOME SCRIPTURE

BIG IDEA: Each of us has a story to share, and sharing our stories helps us come to appreciate each other.

You'll need:

- Copies of the **Sharing Our Stories** handout (page 98)
- Pens
- Bibles

If your group has already done the exercise entitled "Finding Myself in God's Story" (page 47), then begin this conversation by asking: **Do you remember the way we described God's story previously?** Feel free to give hints, such as "You used four words, and they all started with G." See if students can describe Good, Guilt, Grace, and Gratitude in their own words.

OR

If your group didn't do the "Finding Myself in God's Story" exercise, then begin this conversation by asking: **If you had to describe the gospel in your own words, how would you describe it?** Let students share their various descriptions of the gospel.

Explain: **I like describing the gospel by using a story, a story with four different acts.** At this point, distribute Bibles and summarize the descriptions of Good, Guilt, Grace, and Gratitude from pages 47-48. Periodically ask students if they have any questions or comments to add.

THEN TRANSITION TO THE REST OF THIS DISCUSSION...

Continue: **Just as the gospel has a story, so do our own lives. I'm going to distribute a handout that gives you a chance to think about ways you've seen the Good, Guilt, Grace, and Gratitude of the gospel in your own life. On this handout, jot down words, pictures, or even personal stories that overlap with the four acts of the gospel story.** To give your students a sense for what you're looking for, you might consider filling out the handout yourself in advance and sharing ways you've experienced Good, Guilt, Grace, and Gratitude in your own life.

After students have completed their handouts, invite a few volunteers to share what they've written. Make sure you affirm their bravery for sharing as well as the particulars of the gospel story in their own lives.

Ask those who shared: **How did it feel to share your stories?**

Ask those who didn't share: **What new insights did you glean by hearing our friends' stories?**

Q: **How might those insights shape our relationships with one another during our time serving as a team?**

Q: **How might those insights affect our relationships when we get home?**

Expand students' vision for the gospel beyond their team relationships by asking: **In what ways might we see more of the gospel story of Good, Guilt, Grace, and Gratitude in the midst of our service?**

Explain: **Periodically during this trip we're going to hear one another's stories and celebrate how our stories overlap and illustrate the gospel story. Those volunteers who went today get to choose those who will share the next time we gather.** Let those volunteers select the students who will share their stories next and give the group (and those students who will be sharing next) a sense for when your next meeting will be. Continue this process in other meetings throughout your justice work so all team members get to share their stories and celebrate how God's gospel is transforming them.

Close by praying for those students who volunteered today, that they will continue to be sensitive to God's gospel that is working in them and through them.

Take a few minutes to write words, phrases, and stories, and/or draw pictures, that illustrate the overlap between the gospel story of Good/Guilt/Grace/Gratitude and your own life. Be as specific as possible, please.

GOOD: *We were created by a loving God in God's own image.*

When in your life have you sensed God's love for you? How and where do you see evidence of God's image in you?

GUILT: *Sin separates us from our loving God.*

What areas of your life hinder your relationship with God? How does that make you feel?

GRACE: *God sent Jesus so we might have eternal life in the future as well as a better quality of life in the present.*

In what ways does your relationship with Jesus affect your life? How have you experienced Jesus' grace, freedom, or healing power?

GRATITUDE: *Now we serve and obey God out of gratitude for all God has done for us.*

What parts of your life—especially your choices—reflect your gratitude for all God has done for you?

WHY ASK "WHY?"

BY KARA POWELL

BIG IDEA: Meeting the needs of the poor Jesus-style means asking why they are poor in the first place.

You'll need:

- Copies of the *Why Ask "Why?"* handout (page 102), and/or copies of the *Deep Justice Journeys Student Journal* (pages 71-74). If being on the field makes this difficult, figure out another way to give each student a copy of the Camara quotation on the handout. You could possibly read it aloud and ask students to jot it down themselves.

- Pens

- Bibles

- (HAVE MORE TIME? option: Copies of the **Not-As-Deep Service vs. Deep Justice** handout on page 34)

Help students reflect upon the day's experiences by asking the following questions:

Q: **In what ways have you encountered or experienced poverty yourself before this justice journey?**

Q: **What did you see, smell, or hear today that reflected a sense of poverty among the people here?**

Q: **When you encounter people who are poor, how do you feel? What do you tend to think about?**

Q: **What did we do today to help people who are poor?**

Q: **What do you think Jesus would have done for the poor if he were part of our team?**

At this point, distribute the **Why Ask "Why?"** handout and lead students through the questions on the handout.

Explain: **Christians today seem to fall into two camps. One group emphasizes that Jesus called individuals to follow him and then lead a life of personal purity. These Christians tend to focus primarily on the importance of making a personal decision to follow Jesus.**

The second group believes Jesus emphasized serving others and righting wrongs in his name. **This second group tends to focus on what we can and should do to help those who are poor or marginalized. Which of these two perspectives best captures Jesus?**

Let students wrestle with this tough question. The hope is that your students realize that Jesus was—and is—about both calling individuals to follow and worship him *and* being involved in caring for the least, the last, and the lost. If your students don't arrive at this understanding themselves, try nudging them there yourself. Your goal is to affirm that the real Jesus is beyond *either* personal salvation *or* social reform. He transcends this *either/or* by embodying the *both/and* of the two.

Q: **Which of these two positions best describes our church?**

Q: **Which of these two positions best describes your parents?**

Q: **What's good about each of these emphases? What do we lose when we focus on one part of Jesus' message and neglect the other?**

Explain: **We'd have a much deeper understanding of both sides of the kingdom if we grasped God's plan for his creation. Since Genesis 1, God has wanted to establish *shalom* (a Hebrew word pronounced "sha-LOME") over all his people and all creation.**

Shalom **is often translated as "peace," and while that's not a bad translation, we've tended to focus on only a few facets of the peace God intends. We often think of peace as an absence of conflict or some warm-and-fuzzy feeling that everything is going to work out okay. *Shalom* is far more than that. The type of peace God intends has many forms:**

> **Peace with God**
>
> **Peace with other humans**
>
> **Peace with nature**
>
> **Peace with oneself [16]**

HAVE MORE TIME?

Explain to students: **Just like *shalom*, the Greek word *dikaiosune* (pronounced "dih-ky-oh-SUE-nay") has also been misunderstood. In general, this Greek word has been translated in the New Testament gospels and epistles as "righteousness." While that's an accurate translation, it misses the full story. Dikaiosune also means God's just rule, or God's justice.**

In Matthew 5:6, Jesus teaches, "Blessed are those who hunger and thirst for *dikaiosune*, for they will be filled." In Matthew 6:33, Jesus promises, "But seek first his kingdom and his *dikaiosune*, and all these things will be given to you as well." The North American tendency is to think of that type of "righteousness" as an individualistic form of "right living" akin to the warning not to "smoke, drink, chew, or go with those who do."

16. Nicholas Wolterstorff, "The Contours of Justice: An Ancient Call for Shalom," in *God and the Victim: Theological Reflections on Evil, Victimization, Justice, and Forgiveness*, edited by Lisa Barnes Lampman and Michelle D. Shattuck (Grand Rapids: Eerdmans, 1999), 113.

Q: **What happens when we view** *dikaiosune* **as God's justice in these two passages?** Give students time to answer the question and then continue: **Our minds tend to jump to a new form of "right living" that is far more holistic and extends God's kingdom to meet others' spiritual, emotional, social, and physical needs.**

Q: **How, if at all, does that sense of expanded** *shalom* **relate to Dom Helder Camara's quotation?**

Q: **Based on a larger understanding of Jesus' gospel and the kingdom** *shalom,* **what keeps the people we've seen today from experiencing all of God's** *shalom***?**

Q: **What would it look like to ask why the poor have no food in the setting we're in now?**

Q: **What would we gain by asking why? What might we lose?**

Q: **Do you agree that asking why people are poor seems more like communism than Christianity? If so, what does that say about us as Christ-followers?**

HAVE MORE TIME?

If you haven't incorporated it into your discussions earlier, distribute copies of the **Not-As-Deep Service vs. Deep Justice** handout (page 34) to your students for discussion.

Q: **Based on what we've just discussed, how would you like to deepen our service and justice work in…**

…the next 24 hours?

…the next week?

…the next month?

Close in prayer, giving students a chance to pray that they would have the courage to ask why, and that when they do, others will know they aren't communists but Christ-followers.

Dom Helder Camara was a twentieth-century Roman Catholic priest who showed a relentless commitment to justice work among the poor of Brazil. Camara is famous for the following quotation:

"When I feed the poor, they call me a saint. When I ask why the poor have no food, they call me a communist."

1. How would you restate Camara's quotation in your own words?

2. What do you agree with in this quotation? What do you disagree with?

3. If Camara walked up to Jesus and said these two sentences to him, what do you think Jesus would say in response?

MAPPING THE COMMUNITY

BY TERRY LINHART

BIG IDEA: We need to confront our hasty assumptions by learning more about the unique stories that shape and define our host community.

NO
SCRIPTURE

You'll need:

- Copies of the **Mapping Exercises** handout (pages 105-106)
- Two or three maps of the area you are serving. If you can't find maps, skip exercise 1 and focus your team on exercises 2 and 3.
- One large piece of poster paper
- Pens
- Markers
- Paper
- Host people or translators willing to assist with cross-cultural nuances

Before your meeting: Arrange for some key folks in the community you're serving to join you and be interviewed by your group for 30 minutes. Exercise 1 works best if the person(s) interviewed have lived in the community long-term; exercise 2 is designed for interviewing church or ministry leaders; and exercise 3 will work best if the interviewees are successful professionals. Be sure to arrange for translators if needed.

> The mapping exercises in this section could be done BEFORE your justice work if you prefer.

Explain: **Today we're going to get to know this community better. How might knowing more about this community help our justice work?**

Q: **What might happen if we rush into our service work without understanding the community?**

Continue: **As you go about these exercises, please be respectful and listen well—let your host people be your guide. You are not here to "get a job done," but instead to listen and learn. When all the teams are finished, each team will present what they have learned to the rest of the group.** Divide your students into smaller teams and give each team one of the exercises below to complete. Make sure you have at least one host (with translator, if needed) in each team. These exercises are likely to take a few hours, so plan your schedule accordingly.

Since we're giving you three mapping exercises, you actually have a lot of flexibility. You can have all of your team do all the exercises over a period of days, or some of your team do some of them, or all of your team do some of them, or…you get the idea.

When all the teams are finished, invite them to return and share with the rest of the group what they found. Then lead the following discussion:

Q: **What insights stand out as particularly significant or interesting?**

Q: **What are the implications of our findings from these exercises for our justice work?**

Q: **What can we do during the rest of our time here that will help us continue to learn the story of this community and the people who live here?**

To conclude, ask each team to gather again and pray for the community, especially for the needs that emerged during this exercise and the people they met during their study of the community.

HAVE MORE TIME?

If there are missionaries in the area with whom you are not directly partnering, invite them to talk to your group about their story, their work, and what they've observed about the community. Another possibility is inviting a key leader from a local Christian organization to come and share with your group. You may also want to consider bringing in people from the community you're serving who have been to your own community or country and can talk about the contrasts between their own culture and yours.

Another option is to arrange for your students to spend the night at the homes of the folks they interview. This immersion helps make the mapping exercise all the more significant as your students literally walk in the footsteps of your hosts. If you do this, make sure you train your students on appropriate guest etiquette in that culture. In addition, make sure there are at least two students and one adult from your group at each home for safety.

► PAGE 1 ◄

Mapping Exercise 1: Bird's Eye View

What is the layout of the community where you're serving? Using two (or more) maps of the area, draw a new map on the poster paper to share with the rest of the group. On the new map, indicate some of the dynamics related to community infrastructure, including answers to the following questions that you ask your host:

1. **Where did the town first start and how did it grow?**

2. **Are there specific groups of people living in particular sections of the community? Label and mark them on the map.**

3. **Mark on a map where your host church(es) are.**

4. **Where do people in your community gather? What are the "hot spots?"**

5. **Where is housing growing in the community?**

6. **Where is the "rough" or "poorer" area of this community?**

7. **Where do the more wealthy people tend to live?**

8. **What are the locations of the high schools and other schools in the community? What are the differences between the high schools?**

9. **What other places in town are there that people from here recognize?**

To get this new map completed, you will need to spend some more time with some of your host people and let them guide you. Instead of those local people just explaining it to you, it would be best if you went out and walked (or rode) around in order to identify the features of the community yourself. Feel free to mark other aspects of the community that will interest your team on your map.

Mapping Exercise 2: What Has God Been Doing Here?

The goal of your team is to "map" the Christian community in the area. You will need to be very sensitive, as there can be deep divisions between churches that stretch back many years (or sometimes even centuries).

Discuss the questions below with church or ministry leaders. You may not be able to hear all "sides of the story," and that's okay. Remember, sensitivity and relational trust-building are more important than rushing through these questions. If you don't get answers to all the questions, that's okay.

1. **List all the Christian churches (both Protestant and Catholic) in your area.**

2. **What other Christian ministries exist in the area?**

3. **Are there "groups" of churches that connect well with each other? What are those groups?**

▶ PAGE 2 ◀

4. What percentage of the community attends church on the weekends?

5. What stories are there of revivals or key people becoming Christian?

6. What missionaries have come to this community? What missionaries or Christian leaders are still here?

7. Has anyone from this community gone somewhere else as a pastor or missionary?

8. Other than Christian churches, what other religious groups are active in this community? What are these groups like?

Mapping Exercise 3: Who Are the Key Stakeholders?

This exercise invites your team to meet with at least three people from the community who are successful professionals. Each interview should last no more than 30 minutes. Make sure you have a host from your local community with you to help translate and/or pick up on cultural nuances.

As you meet with each person, explain (very briefly) where you're from and what you're doing in the community. When it seems appropriate, move toward interview time, centering on these questions:

1. Can you tell us a little of your story?

2. How did you become involved in your work here?

3. What are some of the unique qualities of this community?

4. What are the economic dynamics of the community?

5. How has the community grown or changed over the years?

6. What have been some other changes you would like to see happen?

7. What misunderstandings might guests (such as us) have about your community?

8. What advice would you have for us, as outsiders, as we serve in this community?

When you are done with your interviews, spend some time as a team summarizing your findings and getting ready to share your insights with the other teams.

"IF YOU'RE HAPPY AND YOU KNOW IT...SMILE"

BY DAVE LIVERMORE

BIG IDEA: When we encounter poverty, we're faced with the challenging task of thinking about the connection between money and happiness.

SOME SCRIPTURE

You'll need:

- Pens
- Bibles

Greet your students and tell them you want to talk about one of the most common statements made by short-term mission teams who encounter poverty. (If you've heard your own students saying something like the following, you can even reference those conversations):

"These people are so happy despite the horrid conditions in which they live. They sing with joy, they serve us better meals than they eat themselves, and they have an overall spirit of contentment."

> Q: **How does this statement relate to your own thoughts and experiences during your justice journey? Have you thought or said something similar to this? Have you heard other people say something like this?**

Affirm that it's very important to realize true happiness isn't the result of having a lot of stuff. It's quite possible for people to be happy, even when they might seem to have far less than we have. Have a volunteer read 1 Timothy 6:6-10 and then ask: **What kind of gain comes from the combination of godliness and contentment?**

> Q: **It's been said that true contentment can come only to a person who has a relationship with Jesus Christ. Do you agree or not? Explain.**

> Q: **Can you think of a time when you felt extremely content and it had nothing to do with money or the things you had? If so, why did you feel content then?**

Given the provocative nature of this exercise, it's especially important to read it carefully in advance before leading students through this conversation. You'll want to make sure you understand the twists and turns of the discussion that might emerge as students think more deeply about their typical responses to poverty.

In *The Message*, Eugene Peterson paraphrases Paul's words from 1 Timothy 6:5-8: "A devout life does bring wealth, but it's the rich simplicity of being yourself before God. Since we entered the world penniless and will leave it penniless, if we have bread on the table and shoes on our feet, that's enough."[17]

---

17. Eugene Peterson, *The Message* (Colorado Springs: NavPress, 2002), 2167.

Having established the biblical precedent for contentment being tied to godliness, stretch your students with a series of questions to help them think more deeply about whether the under-resourced people you're with are happy.

Transition by saying something like: **Let's think a bit more deeply about the people who live here. Would you say the people in this community are happy? Why do you say that?** Students typically respond by talking about the smiles, warmth, and generosity they experience from the locals.

Q: **Since we are visitors here, take some time to think about your own experiences when people come to visit you. How might the emotions you show when someone visits your house or community be similar to the emotions our hosts are showing toward us?** The point is to help students realize that, just as we and our families might become more positive when guests walk into our lives and homes, the locals might be doing the same thing.

Q: **How have you tended to respond to the locals when they smile at us and serve us?** We usually "smile back" and show equal amounts of warmth to the locals.

Q: **So do the smiles we give to people we meet on this justice mission definitely mean we are "so happy"? The point here is not so much to get your students talking about whether they are happy. Instead, the goal is to stretch your students to move beyond the easy assumption that the smiles we encounter are a clear indication that the local people are truly happy. Just as we might assume "Our smiling hosts are happy; therefore poor people are happy," so also the locals might be thinking, "Our smiling guests are happy; therefore rich people from North America are happy." Help them realize that neither conclusion is necessarily true.**

In addition, if there's a language barrier, this is a good time to point out that nervous laughter is often a way of dealing with the awkwardness of not being able to do much more than greet one another.

Q: **Can you think of a time when you were miserable but you put on a happy face for a stranger?** Most of us have all feigned contentment even in the midst of an awful day because our culture has told us we shouldn't divulge everything going on in our inner world to everyone we meet.

Q: **I wonder what some of the cultural norms are here for when people are supposed to appear happy.** See if your students have any ideas based on what they know about the culture.

NOTE: Your point isn't to suggest that the people you encounter on this justice journey can't possibly be happy. They might be happy. But they just as well might NOT be happy. The goal of this discussion is to realize that, apart from deep relationship and lots of understanding, we just don't know someone's level of contentment—especially cross-culturally. Just observing smiling faces and hospitality isn't enough to conclude that poor people are happy. Many of them are longing for some kind of economic relief. Some are experiencing broken relationships (just like us). And the pain of life exists here as it does at home.

Q: **If we simply assume people are "happy" because they smile at us when we're here, how might that affect our commitment to deep justice?** We can too quickly ease our conscience about responding to poverty if we convince ourselves poor people are happy just the way they are.

Conclude this session by affirming the complexity of discerning how money affects people's contentment. But as we learned from Timothy, we can be sure the greatest contentment is found in godliness. Invite a few students to close by praying that the members of your group as well as those you serve would find their ultimate contentment not in what they own, but in godliness. Consider also asking your students to say a quick prayer for discernment whenever locals smile at them, asking that God would help them avoid making quick assumptions.

SMELLS LIKE...

BY DAVE LIVERMORE

NO SCRIPTURE

BIG IDEA: Stopping to notice the sights, sounds, and objects around us can give us new insights into ourselves and others.

You'll need:

- Six to eight large sheets of paper. Ahead of time, title each paper with a different observation prompt mentioned below (e.g., "The dominant sound I hear is..."). Feel free to substitute some of your own based on your group's experiences.
- Markers
- Pens
- Bibles

Begin by asking your group if there's a particular color they think they've seen more than any other this week. Let them take this any direction they want—the color of the dirt, the roofs, the wall you're painting, your group's T-shirts, etc.

Pick one response that names a color they've noticed in the culture (e.g., "red because so many of the roofs are red").

Q: **Why do you think that color is so predominant here?**

Explain: **Taking the time to think about the things we're observing is an important part of learning from our justice work. When we move from observing the color that seems predominant to interpreting why we think that's true, we can't just assume we're right. Instead, we should start testing out our theories; for example, we could ask the locals if they know *why* there is an abundance of red roofs.**

Explain: **There are large sheets of paper and pens scattered throughout the room with different categories written on them. You'll have several minutes to move around to the different sheets to record some of the things you've noticed. Don't overthink your answers. Sometimes your first thoughts are the most profound.**

As you write down your own thoughts, note how your response compares with the response of others. At each paper, feel free to discuss with the others there what you and others have written.

1. The dominant sound I hear is...

2. One smell I've noticed here is...

3. Something I haven't seen here is...

4. Something I see that looks a lot like home is...

5. People's primary purpose here seems to be...

6. The most obvious objects I see are...

7. The youth here are...

Make sure to take down the sheets of paper immediately after your meeting so your local hosts do not see students' raw observations and assumptions, which might be offensive.

After giving students several minutes to go around the room and write their observations, lead the following discussion:

Q: **What did you notice about the types of things written down?**

Q: **What observation by someone else surprised you?**

Q: **What themes do you see in what we have experienced?**

Q: **Did you struggle with knowing what to write? Why do you think you struggled?**

Q: **How well do you think we really know this place and these people? How can we go deeper?**

Encourage students to take one observation (either their own or someone else's) and focus on it tomorrow. After spending a day focused on that observation, see if that observation still feels accurate. Encourage them to find a way to test out *why* a certain thing is true about this place and/or these people. This will likely involve them chatting with locals about what they've noticed, which will likely lead to a deeper understanding of the community you're serving.

Close by inviting students to choose one of the categories posted on paper and to cluster with other students around that sheet. Allow groups time to pray together for better understanding about that particular element of culture.

HAVE MORE TIME?

Have students journal about one observation they've made of something that seems most different from what they would find at home (e.g., if they felt like the primary color here was red and at home was black). Have them write down the differences and what they think the differences might mean.

Encourage students to begin journaling about things they've observed here that they don't want to forget when they're home—including things they've observed about themselves, your group, God, and the local people.

THE FACE OF CHRIST

BY BRAD GRIFFIN

LOTSA SCRIPTURE

BIG IDEA: Serving others can be a sacramental experience through which we encounter the very face of Christ in those we serve, in one another, and even in ourselves.

You'll need:

- Paper
- Pencils
- Bibles
- Elements for Communion—either bread and juice or whatever's available at your site. Try using Communion elements indigenous to where you are serving, like rice or chapattis instead of the traditional bread or wafers your students might be accustomed to.
- (HAVE MORE TIME? option: Small handheld mirrors for each student [cheaply available at most craft stores], or a way students can pass around a mirror or stand in front of one)

Part 1 (Morning Conversation)

Begin by asking students to close their eyes and think about the different faces they've seen in the past 24 hours. Then distribute paper and pencils and invite students to journal silently about these questions as you read them aloud slowly:

> We recommend you do this learning activity in two different gatherings (preferably a morning and then an evening), but you could combine the two discussions into one longer exercise.

Q: **How would you describe the faces you've seen in the past day? What words would you use to describe their appearance...their emotions...their expressions...their reactions?**

Q: **Whose face disturbed you the most? Why do you think you reacted so strongly?**

Q: **Whose face made you smile? Why do you think you reacted so positively to that person?**

Invite a few students to share reflections aloud if they are comfortable doing so. Next ask—

Q: **Why do faces evoke so much response in us? What is it about faces that move us so deeply?** If it doesn't come out in the discussion, be sure to point out we communicate a great deal nonverbally through our facial expressions—possibly more than we communicate through our words.

Q: **Now think about yourself. What do you think others learned about you through your face?**

Q: **Now think about that a different way: What do you think others learned about *Christ* through your face in the past day?**

Q: **How did you experience the face or presence of Christ in others? Why do you think Jesus seemed especially present or powerful in that moment?**

Next read Matthew 25:34-40, in which Jesus says that when we serve people who are considered the "least" by society, we are actually serving Jesus himself.

Q: **Why do you think Jesus was so emphatic that serving people in need is the same thing as serving him?**

Q: **Think back to the faces you saw yesterday. Does it make you think differently about them when you consider that those faces were the very face of Christ?**

Explain: **Throughout the history of the church, certain practices have been considered "sacraments," or ways we experience Jesus' presence and grace through acts of worship. The two main sacraments recognized across almost all Christian traditions are baptism and the Lord's Supper (or Holy Communion). But a number of other experiences also have been considered sacramental in nature. Serving people in need can be one of those kinds of experiences.**

Q: **How could seeing Jesus' face in the poor—or specifically in the folks we are serving—be considered a sacramental experience, meaning a worshipful experience in which we experience God's grace?**

Close your morning discussion by explaining: **In the midst of our justice work today, I would like each of us to remain mindful of how our work, and the people with whom we interact, might be sacramental for us. We'll gather together at the end of the day to share our insights.** Give students time to close in prayer, perhaps journaling their prayers at the bottom of the paper they've been writing on. Consider encouraging them to draw faces—their own or others they've seen during their justice work—in the midst of their prayer journaling.

What makes something "sacramental"? Though denominations and theologians may disagree at points about what constitutes a sacrament, since Augustine, the most commonly held understanding of a Christian sacrament is that it is an "outward and visible sign of an inward and invisible grace." Sacraments are sacred practices that embody our commitment to and fidelity with God and the community of faith. If your own faith tradition would look down on you saying that seeing the face of Jesus in the poor is a "sacramental" experience, then use other language and don't lose your job. You might simply call it what it is: A great mystery.[18]

---

18. See Stanley Grenz, *Theology for the Community of God* (Grand Rapids: Eerdmans, 2000), 511-20, for more on the theology of sacramental practices in the church. To read more reflections on worship, ritual, and identity formation in light of our faith practices within youth ministry, see "Singing ourselves nowhere: the like-it-or-not impact of worship on identity formation," and "Through the Zone: Creating Rites of Passage in Your Church" at www.fulleryouthinstitute.org.

What's necessary in the act of taking Communion? In 1 Corinthians 11:23-26 Paul provides three features: 1. a common meal; 2. remembering the Lord's presence in the acts of taking bread and wine; and 3. pointing to our future hope in the kingdom of God, by continuing this ritual "until he comes."[20] So while our different traditions may place various requirements on the ways Communion should be prepared and taken, these basic features mark the essential spirit of the sacrament.

Part 2 (Evening Conversation)

At the end of the day, gather with your students again and ask: **What did you experience today that felt sacramental?** Be prepared to get the ball rolling and lead by example by sharing sacramental experiences from your own day.

Q: **In what ways did the faces of others help you more thoroughly experience Christ?**

Remind students that Communion is one of the most commonly practiced sacraments and then ask: **How is taking Communion like seeing the face of Christ? How is sharing Communion with others like seeing the face of Christ?**

As we noted earlier, Communion has been an important sacrament of the church since Christ encouraged his followers to celebrate it together. The justice-seeking 20th century priest Henri Nouwen once wrote that our identity in Christ shares the nature of the Lord's Supper. As the Spirit moves in our lives to form us into deeply loved sons and daughters of God, we are "taken, blessed, broken, and given," reflecting the actions of the Lord's Supper.[19] So in a mysterious way, through our faithful surrender to Christ, we become bread for the world as we are taken, blessed, broken, and given by God.

We are now going to share in the Lord's Supper together. As we do, I encourage you to remember that just as these elements of bread and juice represent Christ to us, you and I represent Christ to the world—and specifically right now to the people we are serving.

Share in Communion together, reading from either 1 Corinthians 11:23-26 or Matthew 26:26-29. If it fits your context, you may also want to sing worship songs together. Close your time in whatever prayer format seems most appropriate—in pairs, small groups, or as one large group.

HAVE MORE TIME?

As part of this exercise, invite students to look carefully at their own reflection in a mirror. Have them ponder their own face, and consider how the face of Christ might show through their face, words, and actions. Invite kids to pray while looking at their own face, asking that they might be the very face of Christ to someone in need today (or tomorrow, if you are doing this at night). If you cannot provide a separate mirror for each student, alternative ways to pull this off might be to pass one mirror around or to invite students to take turns coming forward and looking in a mirror during a time of prayer and reflection. You could also weave this into the experience of taking Communion together by having the Communion elements on a table in front of a mirror.

---

19. Henri Nouwen, *Life of the Beloved: Spiritual Living in a Secular World* (New York: Crossroads, 1994), 48-49.

20. Ralph P. Martin, *Worship in the Early Church* (Grand Rapids: Eerdmans, 1964), 122.

EAT IT UP

BY BRAD GRIFFIN

BIG IDEA: Meals as a team can be so much more than functional necessities while we serve; they can become holy moments through our table fellowship.

LOTSA SCRIPTURE

You'll need:

- Bibles
- Elements for Communion—either bread and juice or whatever's available at your site. Don't be afraid to use Communion elements that are indigenous to where you are serving, like rice or chapattis instead of the traditional bread or wafers your students might be accustomed to.

Open by asking students about the food: Their favorite food so far; a local food they're still hoping to try; and maybe what foods from home they are missing. Be sure to be sensitive to the presence of your hosts when you ask these questions. If students have been grumbling about the food, please use discretion in whether to ask these questions at all!

> This discussion could happen during a meal, immediately after a meal, or even just before a meal if you don't have impatient stomachs on your hands. You could also spread it out over the course of a few meals. In any case, this content will be best digested (so to speak) in the context of a meal.

Next ask:

Q: **What is your favorite thing about meals—here, at home, or anywhere?**

Q: **How many of you like eating with others? How many would rather eat alone? What makes a difference in whether you would rather eat alone or with other people?**

Eating is something we do every day—it's essential to life—but we seldom stop to reflect on how important it is that we eat *together*. We eat so we can keep living, but when we do it with others, it's a reminder of our need to be in community with one another. In fact, when we look closely at Scripture we see that eating together is important to us spiritually, too.

Q: **Why do you think eating is spiritually significant? How could sharing a meal be a spiritual encounter?** Note that students may connect the dots differently here depending on whether you have had many conversations about the interconnectedness of our physical and spiritual lives. If you did the "What Do They Need More?" exercise on pages 49-52, you might refer back to that conversation here and ask whether eating can ever be "just" physical or "just" spiritual—or if it's always both.

Q: **What examples from Scripture can you think of that describe people sharing meals that had some sort of spiritual significance?** Likely Jesus' Last Supper will be mentioned, but push them to think about (or suggest yourself) other meals, like Abraham's visit from God (Genesis 18:1-15); the manna and quail God provided for the people in the wilderness (Exodus 16); Elijah's food from ravens (1 Kings 17:6) and from an angel (1 Kings 19:5-8); and Jesus' feeding of the crowds (Mark 6:30-44 and Mark 8:1-13). It has also been noted that Jesus is often eating (or going to a meal, or coming from a meal!) in the gospel of Luke.

"Table fellowship"—the act of eating together—is a powerful symbol across all cultures, often carrying both social and spiritual significance. In Mediterranean cultures in the first century, eating together communicated loyalty and intimacy, and was an act of reconciliation. The Pharisees taught that the table at home was a representation of the altar at Jerusalem—a holy place for worshipping God. In this context, who you ate with said a lot about the kind of person you were. Despite this fact, Jesus always seemed eager to share a meal with just about anyone—so much so that Luke 7:34 reveals that he was sometimes accused of being a glutton and a heavy drinker!

Then say: **Let's look together at one meal in particular that gives us a picture of Jesus' heart for justice and reconciliation through the way he ate his meals.**

Have someone read Mark 2:13-17 and then explain: **By recruiting a tax collector to follow him, Jesus was inviting one of the most hated members of Jewish society to be part of his team. Tax collectors dishonestly levied fees against their own people, often taking more than was required by the Roman occupiers and keeping quite a bit for themselves.**

Q: **What surprises you about this passage?**

Q: **How do you think these people felt about eating with Jesus? Why do you think the religious leaders were so upset?**

You may also point out that tax collectors were not only considered traitors by the people but also declared "unclean" by the Pharisees, which meant they could not attend worship or hang out with other Jews, especially to eat. So Levi's table, according to this context, was a defiled table—an unholy place. Yet we find Jesus eating there! What's more, the text identifies that "many" tax collectors and sinners followed Jesus. It's one thing to walk behind someone along the road, but quite another to sit with him at the table and eat. Jesus' table fellowship with the outcasts of his community was an act of both healing and worship—of making people well and making them holy.

Q: **What do Jesus' eating habits reveal to us about Jesus' perceptions of justice?**

Levi's decision to follow Jesus likely came with quite a cost. Levi would likely never return to his job as tax collector, which was a widely sought-after job because it was considered a sure way to get rich quickly.

Q: **What do you think our own eating habits on this justice mission, both individually and as a group, communicate about God's heart for justice?**

Q: **In light of all of this, what might we want to do differently when we next eat together?** Depending on whether your team eats alone or with locals—or in the case of many mission trips, alone while locals cook and watch—students might bring up uncomfortable feelings or questions about whether it seems just to exclude locals from your table. These are good questions to explore, so be sure you have thought through the implications of changing your eating plans if that's where your group heads in the discussion!

Continue: **Eating together communicates a sense of family-like connectedness. Jesus' common practice of sharing meals with "saints and sinners" alike unveils the value of table fellowship. The Lord's Supper takes this a step further, making it an act of connection with God the Father, Son, and Holy Spirit, and with other believers as we remember Christ's sacrifice.**

Jesus used food—bread and wine—to illustrate his death on the cross. Some Christians believe that every time we eat with other believers, we are announcing Jesus' death and resurrection, and that he will come again. And almost all Christians believe sharing in the act of Communion is a sacred practice. So today we are going to share the Lord's Supper together as part of our meal. This is our act of faithfulness to eat as a community seeking God's justice on earth.

Transition into a time of taking Communion together, or if you are still waiting to eat at this point, begin your meal and then follow it with Communion! At some point during your Communion experience, lead the following discussion:

Psalm 34:8 invites us, "Taste and see that the LORD is good; blessed are those who take refuge in him."

Let's think for a minute about this question: Who else needs to be brought to the table? Whom do you know who desperately hopes to hear an invitation to come and eat, to find themselves at home with Christ, and to taste the new life Jesus offers? You could try to focus students' answers on the people in the community you're serving, or you could encourage them to think about people back home. Perhaps better yet, invite them to think of people in both settings as a way to connect the dots between their current justice work and their life at home.

Community—and Communion—are never just acts we do for ourselves; they should always point us outward to love others more faithfully in the name of Jesus. Let's close in prayer for those who need to experience the good news, both here in the community we're serving or back at home. Let's pray that the way we live—even the ways we eat together—might whet their appetites for Christ.

> The early church used several names for this special meal. Paul called it the "Lord's table" (1 Corinthians 10:21) or the "Lord's Supper" (11:20); and uses the expression *koinonia* for the cup and bread (10:16). *Koinonia* became *communio* in Latin, which became communion in English. So, *koinonia* in the New Testament referred both to Christian fellowship and the Lord's Supper.[21] This combination is important to remember: The act of breaking bread together in table fellowship was both worship and a community ethic, as evidenced in Acts 2:42,46; 20:7,11; and 27:35.

---

21. Werner Elert, *Eucharist and Church Fellowship in the First Four Centuries* (St Louis, Concordia, 1966), 1.

HAVE MORE TIME?

Here are some additional ideas for ways to make community meals more meaningful during your justice work:

- Make it a practice to gather in a circle and pray before meals. While this may seem like a simple thing, the symbol of the circle itself is important imagery of our unity in Christ. Alternate between holding hands, linking arms, standing shoulder-to-shoulder, sitting on the floor, and any other creative way you and your students can think of being together in a circle. Invite the Lord to bring deeper unity as you begin each meal this way, and point out to students the reason you make circles together.

- Occasionally assign seats or require that students sit next to someone new at a meal. While meals can be important downtime for students to hang with their closest friends, this can also inhibit deeper relationships from forming across group lines. If possible, plan at least a few (if not all) meals for students to intentionally eat with locals as well.

- If your meals are not already set up this way, consider involving students in preparing, serving, and cleaning up after each meal.

- If you usually eat in a private space as a team, consider going to a local restaurant or somewhere you can eat among others in the community. Or find a way to make and serve food for the church or ministry you are working with, as an expression of gratitude and solidarity with your hosts.

- Occasionally make new meal rules, like restricting use of hands during a meal so everyone has to be fed by someone else near them, or that each person can only use the hand that is opposite their normal preference.

YOUR KINGDOM COME

BY BRAD GRIFFIN

DEVOTION
friendly

LOTSA
SCRIPTURE

BIG IDEA: The prayer Jesus taught his followers can be more than just a tradition we learn from our church and from Scripture—it can catalyze us for living as kingdom people who see God's will being done through our lives.

You'll need:

- Bibles or copies of the Prayer of Jesus from Matthew 6:9-13
- Additional items based on the options you choose below—this one can be as high-prep or as low-prep as you want!

Begin by asking:

Q: **What things did you see today that made you want to pray, or when did you find yourself praying about something you saw or experienced?**

Q: **What kinds of prayers do you find yourself praying here? How, if at all, are your prayers here different from the way you pray at home?**

Q: **How many of you are familiar with what's commonly known as the Lord's Prayer? Can someone say the opening line for us?**

Q: **What else do you know about this prayer?**

Q: **Why do you think this is called the Lord's Prayer? Does that sound like an appropriate title to you? Do you think this should be the only—or the primary—way we pray to God? Why or why not?** You may want to point out that groups of Christians have interpreted this prayer differently through the ages. Some see this as a "perfect" prayer, while others see it as one—but not the only—way to approach God.

> You may dive into this exercise differently based on your church's tradition regarding what's known commonly as the Lord's Prayer in most Protestant churches or the Our Father in Catholic churches. You obviously have a better idea than we do of your students' familiarity with this prayer—whether they've prayed it a thousand times or none. So feel free to adapt this exercise to suit your group. The point of this discussion is to lead into a time of prayer, so we encourage you to leave a significant amount of time to actually PRAY together.

However we view this particular prayer, there is nothing "magic" about saying these words. Prayer is a mysterious interaction with God through which we—and sometimes, but not always, our or others' circumstances—are changed. We cannot pretend to have this all figured out, and we need to help students live within this tension as well.

Continue: **Let's read the verses of this prayer from Scripture and use them as the focus of our time together today.**

Have someone read Matthew 6:9-13 aloud—or read it together if you all have the same translation.

Say: **Today we're going to explore the Lord's Prayer, perhaps in a different way than you've done before, by praying through it phrase by phrase.**

Depending on how much time you have, you may also want to share a few of these notes about Jesus' prayer:

- God is named and described several specific ways in this prayer: As Father, as Holy, and as King. Talk about the ways these names and descriptions impact the way we pray. Specifically, note the intimacy of addressing God as "Father" in prayer. While Jesus models praying to "Our Father in heaven" in Matthew 6:9, *Father* was not a typical word used in that era to address God. Until Jesus, it was considered too familiar and presumptuous. Yet by using the phrase "in heaven," Jesus also reminds his disciples then, and us today, of God's transcendence.

- "Bring the kingdom…" is our primary request in this prayer, which has a sidekick: "Your will be done" (or "We want what you want"). Both have to do with orienting ourselves toward the kingdom of God and submitting ourselves to the reign and desires of God in our midst. These two petitions are the context for the rest of the prayer, as we ask God to:

  - Provide enough for today.

  - Forgive us, and shape us to be people who forgive.

  - Deliver (set us free) from all that is not the kingdom around us.

> The book of Psalms is one example of the wide range of prayers faithful people have lifted to God through the centuries, including complaints, laments, and prayers of celebration and praise. Jesus' own prayers model various ways to interact with God, from simple prayers of thanksgiving (Matthew 14:19) to his agonizing prayer in Gethsemane that God would take away the cup of death from him (Matthew 26:39,42).

> You might want to point out that the first half of the Lord's Prayer focuses mostly on God's glory, while the second half revolves around God's activity on our behalf. The Lord's Prayer also appears in Luke 11:2-4 in shorter form.

Q: **Who is the "us" in this prayer?**

Q: **When you read these words in light of our interactions with the people we are serving—and people who are poor and oppressed all over the world—how do you feel? Does it change the way you pray "Your kingdom come" or "Give us today our daily bread"?**

Q: **How is that different from praying and thinking about yourself, or even about your family or our youth group?**

Q: **What do you think it's like for someone who is literally starving to ask for enough bread for one day at a time? What's it like for someone who is being abused on a daily basis to pray about forgiving others' sins? How might such situations change the meaning and relevance of this prayer?**

Q: **What kinds of action might this prayer lend itself to?**

Next move into a time of corporate prayer. You may want to include one or more of the following ideas every morning or evening for several days in a row:

- Have a leader start each phrase of the prayer as a prompt, then let students continue from there—either silently, vocally, or on paper in words or images—finishing each phrase with prayers specifically about the people you're encountering every day in your host community. Do this phrase by phrase through the prayer.

- Have students split into groups to discuss and then pray over a particular line or theme found in the Lord's Prayer. Then come back together to have each group report on what that was like and what insights they gained as they discussed and prayed through that particular element together.

- Consider using some of these questions for contemplation during prayer, asking them slowly and allowing silent space for students to reflect on each one: **What do we really mean when we pray, "Your kingdom come"? What about, "Your will be done on earth as in heaven"? What images come to mind when we say those words? If we began each day with a prayer such as, "God, bring your kingdom and your will more into focus around me today," how do you suspect we might approach life differently? How do you think those kinds of prayers might change the community we're serving right now?**

Close by asking your group to commit together to practicing this kind of prayer for the rest of your trip, or even over the next month. Encourage students to reflect and journal on the difference it makes in their perspectives, attitudes, feelings, actions, and decisions each day, and to bring those reflections back to share with the group.

HAVE MORE TIME?

Create your own communal prayer (sometimes called a "litany") based on this prayer that includes specific petitions for those affected by poverty, and/or specific prayers for people in your host community, as well as other global and local concerns. Maybe include a corporate refrain like "Your will be done," or "Bring your kingdom, Lord" that the group repeats after each petition. You might pass out slips of paper that have specific prayers for students to lift up at appropriate times, or invite students ahead of time to lead specific parts of the prayer. Or have students get in groups and write these prayers, then pray them all together as an act of worship.

HEROES

BY KARA POWELL

**SOME
SCRIPTURE**

BIG IDEA: Jesus' brand of heroism is different from today's.

You'll need:

*   Bibles

Begin your discussion by sharing about any heroes you had growing up and then ask: **How about you? Who were some of your heroes when you were a kid?**

Q: **What about them seemed heroic to you at that age?**

Q: **Who are the heroes of our culture today?**

Q: **It's been said that instead of heroes, we now have people who are famous. What's the difference? Do you agree with this statement?**

Q: **What acts of heroism did you see today?**

Q: **Do you think the locals would describe our justice work here as heroic? Why or why not?**

Q: **In what ways are the locals we've come to know heroic?**

Q: **In what ways is Jesus heroic?**

Explain: **When Jesus showed up on earth in the first century, the Jewish people were looking for a hero. They had been under Roman oppression and were looking for a strong, military leader (think "Braveheart") who would bring freedom from the Romans. Enter Jesus...**

Jesus' brand of heroism didn't fit what the people were expecting. Let's see how Jesus himself described his mission. At this point, read Luke 4:14-21.

Q: **What words stand out to you from Jesus' proclamation?**

Q: **What do these words about the poor, the prisoners, the blind, and the oppressed tell you about Jesus' brand of heroism?**

Continue: **To see how the people responded to Jesus' words, let's keep reading.** At this point, read Luke 4:22-23.

Initially, people thought Jesus' brand of heroism would be right up their alley—but within minutes, they realized Jesus was bowling on a different lane. At this point read Luke 4:24-29 and explain: **Jesus' references to Elijah helping the widow of Zarephath and Naaman the Syrian would have infuriated his listeners because those two were non-Israelites. God had sent Elijah to spread God's work outside immediate Israelite culture, and similarly, God was now sending Jesus to spread God's kingdom beyond the immediate Jewish culture. Having heard about this expansion, how did the Jews in the synagogue respond?**

Q: **In what ways would it be good for God's kingdom to be expanded here where we're serving?**

Q: **What could we do tomorrow that would be heroic by Jesus' standards of expanding the kingdom in these ways?**

Q: **When Jesus refused to be the kind of hero people were expecting, it nearly got him tossed off a cliff. What might following Jesus' definition of heroism cost us? What might we gain?**

Invite students to gather in pairs for a closing prayer time, praying that the Lord would help us embody Jesus-style heroism in expanding the kingdom in new territory tomorrow.

WHEN I GROW UP, I WANT TO BE...

BY KARA POWELL

SOME SCRIPTURE

BIG IDEA: Our justice mission can—and should—impact the way we think about our future jobs.

You'll need:

- Copies of the **Millennium Development Goals** handout (page 127-128), and/or copies of the *Deep Justice Journeys Student Journal* (page 93-98)

- Bibles

- (HAVE MORE TIME? option: Paper, pencils, and crayons)

Ask students to share what stood out in the day for them, and then transition to the topic of work by asking: **What kinds of work have you observed people in our host community doing?**

Q: **What jobs that you are used to seeing at home are noticeably missing?**

Q: **If you were a teenager living here, what do you think you would want to do when you became an adult? How does that compare with what you want to pursue as a future career in your own country?**

At this point share any memories you have of your own thinking about your future career when you were a high school student. If you were interested in certain jobs, explain why those jobs were so appealing to you. Did you end up in the job you envisioned or did you end up walking down a different career path?

Q: **What is it that makes some jobs appeal to you more than others?**

Reflect aloud: **I wonder how the fact that we are followers of Jesus should impact the way we choose jobs.** Identify any comments students have made up to this point that reflect their faith. If there haven't been many comments up to this point, note that aloud.

Q: **What are some of the needs we've seen firsthand today?**

Q: **What jobs help meet those needs?**

Q: **Are there ways in which the career you hope to pursue can help meet the needs of the people you're serving?**

Q: **What other types of employment might help meet those needs?**

HAVE MORE TIME?

Explain: **Although Jesus was in his 30s when he began his public ministry, Scripture doesn't say much about his job(s) before that time. Since his father, Joseph, was a carpenter, we can assume Jesus worked as a carpenter, too. Think for a moment about Jesus being a carpenter.** Give students 10 to 15 seconds to reflect, and then continue: **What images came to your mind as you thought of Jesus as a carpenter?** Depending on how much time you have, consider distributing paper and pencils (and crayons if you have any) and let students draw the images that came to their minds.

Q: **How would Jesus' work be different from an "ordinary" carpenter's?**

Q: **How would Jesus treat his co-workers?**

Q: **How would Jesus treat his customers?**

Q: **In what ways would Jesus' job as a carpenter give him opportunities to show his love for people and meet their needs?**

At this point, distribute Bibles and invite your students to turn to Colossians 3:17 and ask for a volunteer to read it aloud. Ask: **What do you think Paul means when he writes, "Whatever you do, whether in word or deed, do it all in the name of the Lord Jesus"? What are some practical ways we could live this out?** While there are various interpretations of that phrase, the most accurate is likely that, as believers, we act as Christ's representatives in all we do.

Q: **In what specific ways did we represent Christ today?**

Q: **It's been said that, as followers of Christ, we're always his representatives—it's just that we sometimes make choices that don't represent him very well. Do you agree or disagree? Please explain your answer.**

Q: **What are some ways the jobs you're contemplating for your future can make a deep impact by representing Christ?**

At this point, distribute the **Millennium Development Goals** handout and review the brief history at the top of the flyer. Lead the following discussion:

Q: **How many of you have heard of these Millennium Development Goals (or MDGs) established by the United Nations?** Chances are good it won't be many, so ask: **Why do you think so few of us have heard of these goals?**

Q: **Which of these goals, if met, would make the most difference in the lives of people we've been serving today?**

Q: **Which of the jobs we've discussed today help make progress in one or more of these goals? Why do you think that?**

Q: **The initial vision for these goals was that they would be fulfilled by 2015, which isn't very far away. Imagine that the United Nations is coming to you in 2015 to help them set new goals. Given what you know about the world, which goal categories from this sheet (as well as other world needs you know about) would you suggest after 2015?** This discussion will probably be most helpful if you keep students focused on the eight overall categories and not the individual goals within those categories.

Q: **Based on the goals you've just suggested, in what other ways can the jobs we've mentioned to-day represent Christ by alleviating the suffering of people and offering deep justice around the world? Which kinds of jobs seem noticeably missing from the local community here that could help accomplish the MDGs?**

Q: **How do you think our work here might contribute toward meeting the MDGs?**

At this point, re-read Colossians 3:17 and help students apply it to how they'll be serving tomorrow by asking: **How can we live out Colossians 3:17 in the ways we treat one another tomorrow?**

Q: **How about in the ways we treat the locals tomorrow?**

Lead students through a closing prayer time in which you walk them through the various experiences they're likely to have tomorrow. Name the experience and then give them a few seconds to pray that the Lord will help them be his representative in that moment, and then name the experience that's likely to come next. For instance, mention, "Waking up and getting ready" and then give them a moment to pray about that time. Then say, "Having breakfast," and give students a similar amount of time. Proceed through your day, all the way until students turn out the lights tomorrow night.

MILLENNIUM DEVELOPMENT GOALS

In 2000, the member states of the United Nations agreed to work together to see the following Millennium Development Goals accomplished by 2015. So far progress toward these goals has been mixed. Much remains to be done.

The eight goal categories and the specific targets in each area are as follows:

Eradicate Extreme Poverty and Hunger

- Reduce by half the proportion of people living on less than a dollar a day.
- Reduce by half the proportion of people who suffer from hunger.

Achieve Universal Primary Education

- Ensure that all boys and girls complete a full course of primary schooling.

Promote Gender Equality and Empower Women

- Eliminate gender disparity in primary and secondary education preferably by 2005, and at all levels by 2015.

Reduce Child Mortality

- Reduce by two-thirds the mortality rate among children under five.

Improve Maternal Health

- Reduce by three-quarters the maternal mortality ratio.

Combat HIV/AIDS, Malaria, and Other Diseases

- Halt and begin to reverse the spread of HIV/AIDS.
- Halt and begin to reverse the incidence of malaria and other major diseases.

http://www.un.org/millenniumgoals/

Ensure Environmental Sustainability

- Integrate the principles of sustainable development into country policies and programmes; reverse loss of environmental resources.

- Reduce by half the proportion of people without sustainable access to safe drinking water.

- Achieve significant improvement in the lives of at least 100 million slum dwellers, by 2020.

Develop a Global Partnership for Development

- Develop further an open trading and financial system that is rule-based, predictable, and nondiscriminatory, includes a commitment to good governance, development, and poverty reduction—nationally and internationally.

- Address the least developed countries' special needs. This includes tariff- and quota-free access for their exports; enhanced debt relief for heavily indebted poor countries; cancellation of official bilateral debt; and more generous official development assistance for countries committed to poverty reduction.

- Address the special needs of landlocked and small island developing states.

- Deal comprehensively with developing countries' debt problems through national and international measures to make debt sustainable in the long term.

- In cooperation with the developing countries, develop decent and productive work for youth.

- In cooperation with pharmaceutical companies, provide access to affordable essential drugs in developing countries.

- In cooperation with the private sector, make available the benefits of new technologies—especially information and communications technologies.

SAYING GOOD-BYE WELL

BY TERRY LINHART

BIG IDEA: Saying an appropriate good-bye is an important part of our cross-cultural service experience.

LOTSA SCRIPTURE

You'll need:

- Copies of the **Saying Good-Bye** handouts (page 131-132), and/or copies of the *Deep Justice Journeys Student Journal* (page 99-101)
- Whiteboard or poster paper
- Pens
- Paper
- Pencils
- Bibles

> Here are some "good-bye" examples for you, the leader: *Later, 'Gator; Toodles; Hasta la vista; TTFN; So long; Time to bounce; Let's boogie; See you on the flip side; Catch you later; Aloha; Adios; and Adieu.*

Divide your group into equal teams of four to 10 students and play "The Good-bye Game." Distribute paper and pencils and explain: **I am going to give your team three or four minutes to list different words or phrases people have used to say good-bye. You can write down movie or television quotations, words for good-bye from other languages, or catch phrases you've heard. Brainstorm as many as you can and have one team member write them down.**

At the end of three or four minutes, interrupt the brainstorming and explain: **Starting with the team to my left, and then going around to the other teams one at a time, your team needs to stand and say one of the "good-bye phrases." We'll go around the room until a team cannot come up with a NEW phrase, at which time that team is out.** Be sure to keep the game moving from group to group as quickly as possible. You are the final judge as to whether a phrase is acceptable or not. It's okay if teams come up with phrases as the game progresses. Feel free to award a prize, if appropriate.

Transition by asking: **How does your family say good-bye?**

Q: **What are some "wrong" ways to say good-bye?**

Continue: **Saying good-bye is not as big a deal in some families as in others. In fact, you may have heard someone say, "I hate saying good-bye." However, in most cultures, saying an appropriate good-bye is an important moment. In your teams, think through the following questions:**

1) **What could we unintentionally communicate to others if we do a poor job of saying good-bye during this justice journey?**

2) **Who are the people here to whom we most need to do a good job of saying good-bye?**

Give your teams a few minutes to huddle up and answer those questions and then ask them to share their responses with the entire group.

Distribute Bibles and the **Saying Good-Bye** handouts and invite students to complete the top portion on their own. When they are finished, they can complete the rest in teams.

After each team is done filling out the form, pull everyone back into a large group and have teams share their answers to each question. Make sure to get every group sharing as often as possible, but keep it moving. Write answers to the last question on your whiteboard or poster paper.

Ask the entire group: **How is this scene in Acts 20 the same as saying good-bye to the local people we've worked with on this project?**

Q: **How is it not the same?** One important difference to note might be that your team's visit probably wasn't the first introduction of the gospel to the community.

Q: **What does it mean when we're sad to leave?**

Q: **Since we've shared this intense experience, do we need to think about how to say good-bye to one another as well? If so, how?**

Conclude by distributing paper and explaining: **Working in your teams, I want you to spend the next four or five minutes writing down ideas about how we can say good-bye well on this project. As you're brainstorming, use the three examples in the New Testament listed on your Saying Good-Bye handout as a springboard for your ideas.**

After five minutes invite teams to share their answers. If appropriate, see if your group can choose one or two ideas that stand out to them as the best ways to say good-bye. If you feel like you need more time to consider, massage, or nuance your students' ideas, you can say something like: **I'll think about all these ideas and get back to you with a few possibilities.**

Lay out some poster paper and distribute pens to your students. Invite them to create a good-bye card or picture to present to the church and/or community you've been serving. Brainstorm any Scripture passages you might want to include. If appropriate, make the card a "thank-you" card for all you've learned from the local people.

Close in prayer, inviting students to lift up the names of the local people to whom it will be hard to say good-bye. Ask God to continue to do great kingdom work in the community you're serving, as well as in your community back home.

> Paul's good-bye to the Ephesian elders in Acts 20:17-38 is similar to the format of many of his letters, in that its body has three main components: The past, the present, and the future.

> Saying good-bye well requires cultural sensitivity. It may be tempting to want to give money or to say good-bye in a way that gets the locals to like you or appreciate you more. It will be VERY helpful to talk with someone who understands the cultural dynamics about appropriate good-byes.

SAYING GOOD-BYE

On Your Own

Put an "X" below at the spot that best describes how you feel about good-byes.

⟵───────────────────────────────────────⟶

I don't
mind them.

I haven't thought
much about them.

I don't
like them.

Write down one moment you remember in which you, or someone you know, didn't say good-bye very well.

How did people (including you!) feel when that happened?

With Your Team

Look up the following Scripture verses one at a time and then write down your best answers. Each passage reflects a different "good-bye" in the New Testament:

1. Luke 9:61. The word for *good-bye* in this verse means "to dismiss with orders." Write down times when someone might give instructions as part of their good-bye.

2. Philippians 4:4. The word for *rejoice* also was used for *good-bye*. Write down ways a good-bye can be a really joyful time.

The apostle Paul provides a great example of taking time to say good-bye well. In the midst of his third missionary journey around the Mediterranean, Paul says good-bye to the elders in Ephesus in Acts 20:17-38.

Pick a team member to read verses 17-21 and then discuss: **What did Paul remember about his relationship with the Ephesian elders?**

Have someone read verses 22-27 and then discuss: **What was Paul's main concern in the present?**

Have another team member read verses 28-32 and then discuss: **How did Paul want them to get ready for the future?**

Each person can silently read verses 33-38. Then discuss together: **What does Paul model for us in the way he says good-bye?**

AFTER:
INITIAL DEBRIEF

Taking some time as our justice work comes to a close to cement all that's been learned and experienced…

HIGHLIGHTS FOR HOME

BY TODD BRATULICH

NO SCRIPTURE

BIG IDEA: Sharing your experience helps you process what you've learned and lets others know what God has done and is doing.

You'll need:

- Plain white paper plates
- Crayons or markers
- Copies of the **Highlights for Home** and **Sharing the Highlights** handouts (pages 136 and 137), and/or copies of the *Deep Justice Journeys Student Journal* (page 104-107)
- Pens

Heads up: If you're interested in doing the "Rewind and Fast Forward" activity on page 191, make sure you record (either on audio or video) at least one of your team's debriefing discussions. You might also keep the paper-plate drawings students make in this exercise as a helpful reminder of how students experienced God's transformation of them during their justice journey.

Welcome students and invite them to grab a paper plate and a few markers or crayons. Explain: Today we're going to create pictures of what we experienced during our recent justice work. On one side of your paper plate, I want you to draw a picture of the experience from an outside perspective. In other words, think of what you saw, the people you met, and the things you did that stand out to you. If you want, you could chart your justice journey like a map by listing or drawing the experiences that most impacted you from start to finish.

On the other side of your paper plate, I want you to draw your experience from an internal perspective. In other words, draw about how your experiences made you feel, the new things you learned about, as well as how God shaped or changed your heart. If you'd like, you can also chart your own internal experiences by using a map. After we all finish, I'm going to invite all of you who want to share your pictures or maps to do so. You certainly don't have to, so don't let the thought that you might show your picture to others constrain your honesty or creativity.

Give students 10 to 15 minutes to draw. When they are finished, ask if people would like to share one or both of their drawings. When students are finished sharing, lead the following discussion:

Q: **Did anything surprise you or stand out as you recalled the significant people, places, moments, events, and feelings from our service work?**

Q: **Right now, we're discussing our experiences with others who shared them with us. But as we transition home, we will be sharing our experiences with others who didn't take part in the experience with us. Will that be difficult for you to do? Why or why not?**

Continue: **The transition back home from your mission trip is difficult in many ways, but sometimes the hardest part is figuring out how to share it with others who haven't lived it with us. But figuring out how to share our service highlights is important because it helps us process what we've learned and creates opportunities for others to hear what God has done through our experience.**

Distribute copies of the **Highlights for Home** handout and pens/pencils to students and let them answer its questions.

When students are finished, continue: **Now that you've had some time to think through your experience and how it has impacted you, let's take some time to think about how you will communicate your experience to others. It is often helpful to think of a few different types of responses based on the situation in which you will be sharing.**

Distribute the **Sharing the Highlights** handout and review it together. Give students a few minutes to write a few notes on the front or back of the handout that would help them share their 30-second and their three-minute highlights. Encourage them to take some more time to think about who might benefit from hearing the whole enchilada. Once students have had a chance to write their highlights (or at least some sort of notes or outline), ask if anyone would like to share their three-minute version with the group.

Close in prayer but instead of having students close their eyes, encourage them to keep their eyes open and to look at the drawings they made earlier. Invite students to pray aloud that God would help them continue to process all their experiences, and that God would use these justice highlights to impact those around them.

> Encourage students to share their 30-second and three-minute highlights with their parent(s). It's a great way for students to practice, and it gives parents a chance to hear their own kid's stories.

1. What did you learn about yourself during your journey?

2. What new things did you learn about God?

3. What did you learn from people in the community?

4. Who/what do you specifically want to pray for after you return home?

5. How are you a different person now compared with when you signed up for this justice work?

6. How do you want our youth group to be involved in service at home?

7. When you think of your mission trip, what is one specific "snapshot" that comes to mind?

SHARING THE HIGHLIGHTS

THE 30-SECOND HIGHLIGHT: When people ask the quick question, "How was your trip?" in passing, don't just settle for typical quick responses like "Good" or "It was fun." Think of a two- or three-sentence response that would tell them about something significant you learned or someone significant you met. Your 30-second response might even pique their interest and cause them to ask more questions!

THE THREE-MINUTE HIGHLIGHT: You may be asked to share about your mission experience at youth group, a family gathering, over a meal, or even in a class. If you've only got a couple minutes, it's better to share one meaningful moment or story and what God taught you through it, rather than rushing through all the details of the entire trip or event.

THE WHOLE ENCHILADA: Everybody needs at least one opportunity to unload all the details, emotions, funny highlights, and meaningful memories of their service experience. We encourage you to find at least two people (an adult and a friend your age) who were not with you on the trip and invite them into your experience by telling them your highlights and showing them your pictures. Sharing about how your views of God, yourself, and others were changed during your justice work will help you process your experience and also help those close to you understand how you've been impacted by the experience. It may even help them to see the world, themselves, and God in a different perspective.

Adapted from YouthWorks! 2007 Devotional Journal. Used with permission.

MUSTARD SEEDS AND YEAST

BY APRIL L. DIAZ

SOME SCRIPTURE

BIG IDEA: The kingdom of God is bigger than we think.

You'll Need:

- Copies of the **Then and Now** handout (page 140), and/or copies of the *Deep Justice Journeys Student Journal* (page 108-110)
- Posterboard or a large piece of paper
- Bibles
- Mustard seeds (if possible—if not, use small pebbles or grains of sand instead)
- Bread, preferably freshly baked
- Paper
- Pens

Begin the discussion by asking: **What is your favorite reality TV makeover show?**

Q: **These days there are so many shows that contrast what someone or something was like THEN (before some dramatic transformation) with what it's like NOW. What makes these shows so popular?**

Explain: **In many ways we're experiencing our own THEN and NOW during this justice work. I'm going to give you 10 minutes to consider what you thought God and involvement in his kingdom were like THEN, prior to this justice work. I'd like you to contrast that with what you think God and his kingdom are like NOW that you've been serving others. Distribute the Then and Now handout and pens so students can write down specific views they had THEN and contrast that with their perspective NOW that they've been serving.**

When students are finished, invite them to share some of their "THEN" kingdom perspectives, and write them on the posterboard. Next invite students to share their "NOW" kingdom perspectives. Ask students to identify any themes they see among their THEN perspectives, as well as their NOW perspectives.

Next, invite a student to read aloud Jesus' description of the kingdom of God in Luke 13:18-21. Pass out to each student and leader a mustard seed (or some other tiny object that represents a mustard seed, such as a grain of sand or a small pebble) and a piece of bread.

Q: **In what ways are mustard seeds and yeast helpful images for the kingdom of God? Some possible answers include:**

Our eyes may not show us the full potential of how God is working in and through someone;

God uses the small or insignificant things of this world to make a difference;

God's kingdom is unstoppable;

a small act can have a huge impact.

Q: **How has the kingdom of God become "greater" (expanded) for you during this trip?**

Close in prayer, asking students to begin by placing their hands a few inches apart (palms up) in a time of confession of some of the ways they've minimized the power of the kingdom and its role in their lives. After a few minutes, ask students to open their arms broadly (without knocking over their neighbor) and invite God to continue to show them how GREAT his kingdom is. Ask God to work through your students so his kingdom impact continues to expand both here in the midst of your service as well as when you get home.

> Feel free to use this last question about the kingdom of God as an ongoing theme for your group in the weeks and months to come. Keep a running list of the ways God is expanding your group's perspective of God's kingdom. Let it be a source of encouragement how God is stretching your perspective and how he is using your group to expand God's kingdom!

HAVE MORE TIME?

If you are still in the community where you've been serving, give students a chance to take a short walk (in pairs or small groups for safety, ideally with an adult), noting things they see that sprouted up from something small. That might include flowers, bushes, trees, or a house that started as a pile of lumber. After students have finished their short walks, bring them back together to debrief what they saw, and discuss how their observations relate to the power of the yeast and the mustard seed.

I used to think God was like...

I used to view myself as...

I used to view my family as...

I used to think of my friends as...

I used to view my problems as...

I used to view my future as...

I used to view people who don't know Jesus as...

I used to think of the world as...

Now I realize God is...

Now I view myself as...

Now I view my family as...

Now I realize my friends are...

Now I view my problems as...

Now I view my future as...

Now I view them as...

Now I realize that the world is...

CLASS SEPARATION— DON'T KNOW, OR DON'T CARE?

BY KURT RIETEMA

BIG IDEA: As we identify the class separations in the community we served, as well as in the community where we live, we can seek justice more effectively.

SOME SCRIPTURE

You'll need:

- Bibles
- Paper
- Pens

Begin this discussion with the following questions:

Q: **How would you define *social class*?**

Q: **What have you observed about social class through the people you've met and the experiences you've had in the midst of our justice work?**

Q: **How visible were the social class differences during your service?**

Q: **In what ways could you sense class separation?** (e.g., ethnicity, language, dress, geography)

Q: **In what ways (if any) did you observe any tension or resentment between people of different social classes?**

Q: **What do you think might have caused those conflicts?** (e.g., religion, ethnic identity, different values, job status, prior conflicts)

This discussion will work best if your mission experience includes a "break" in which you spent a few hours, a half day, or a full day away from your "service" to enjoy time relaxing, sightseeing, or shopping. If you're planning to take that type of "break" anyway, you can use this exercise as a catalyst for a deeper understanding of social class and the contrast between those you interacted with when you were serving and those you interacted with during your day of leisure and tourism. If you are not taking that sort of time away from your service work, skip the questions about the "break."

The next five questions invite your group to reflect on its experience while taking a break from service to relax, sightsee, and/or shop. Skip these questions if you didn't take any time off.

Q: What was the highlight of the recent "break" we took?

Q: How were the locals we interacted with during our "break" similar to those we interacted with during our service? How were they different?

Q: After spending most of our time working alongside the poor for justice in this community, how did you feel about stepping into this other world?

Q: Some of you might have been deeply troubled by the contrasts between our experiences, our surroundings, or the social class of the people we interacted with during our "break" as opposed to during our service work. What are some of these differences, and why did you find them disturbing?

Q: Others of you might not have considered these contrasts, and perhaps that fact is troubling you now. Does anyone feel like that? Can you please share your thoughts and feelings with us?

Transition to thinking about social class at home by explaining: We may not have the same extremes of wealth and poverty at home that we've experienced here, but class structures exist at home, too. In what ways do you see class divisions in our town?

Q: How about in your school?

Q: How does social class affect which people you do or don't talk with at school? Why is that?

Q: What, if anything, is good about these different levels of class? What troubles you about these divisions?

Q: As followers of Jesus, how should we respond to the differences among the divisions in social class hierarchies?

Invite a student to read Galatians 3:26-28 and then lead the following discussion:

Q: According to Paul, what happens to our social status after we become children of God through faith in Jesus Christ?

In Paul's day, there was enormous division between the Jews and the Gentiles, meaning people who were not Jewish and therefore not "children of Abraham."

Q: And yet we still are male and female, and other social divisions still exist. So what do you think Paul means?

Q: What would a world, a community, or a church look like that lived out Galatians 3:26-28?

Q: If you were to rewrite Galatians 3:26-28 so it spoke directly to the situation of the locals we served, what would you say? Distribute paper and pencils so students can actually write out the passage.

Q: How would you rewrite that same passage of Scripture for your own school? Invite students to actually write out their version on paper.

Q: How are your versions for the locals and for your school similar? How are they different?

At this point, ask students to get into small groups by either their school or by their grade (depending on how many schools and/or grades you have represented in your group). After they are in small groups, invite students to read aloud to their group the versions of Galatians 3:26-28 they've written for kids in their school. Then give small groups a few minutes to pray that the Lord would break down social divisions in their schools and/or in their grades, just as Paul describes in Galatians. Ask that God would fill you with the grace and courage to move past social lines, even when to do so might be costly.

BACK TO THE "REAL WORLD"

BY KURT RIETEMA

NO SCRIPTURE

BIG IDEA: On mission trips, students often see the "real world" in ways they've never seen it before, including the *real* truth about poverty or glimpses of the *real* kingdom of God. This is the "real world" of following Jesus that we can continue to live out every day.

You'll need:

- Bibles
- Pencils
- Paper

Begin the discussion by asking:

Q: **What have you missed about your life at home while you've been away?**

Q: **We often refer to life back home as the "real world." Why do we call it that?**

Q: **If life back home is the "real world," then what should we label the life we've experienced during our justice work?**

Q: **If we asked Jesus which of these worlds (the world where we've been serving or the world back home) is the "real world," what do you think he would say?**

Q: **If you wanted to make the case that the world we've experienced as we've served is actually more "real" than our world back home, what would you say?**

Q: **In what ways have we seen the "real" Jesus as we've served?**

Q: **In what ways have we seen the "real" church, either among ourselves or among the local people?**

Q **In what ways have we seen "real" relationships?**

Q: **In what ways have we seen "real" grace?**

Continue: Justice work can sometimes give us a different idea of what it really means to follow Jesus and be part of the kingdom community. If that happens, we have at least three potential responses:

1. CONSUME. We can go home with a couple of cheap souvenirs and say to ourselves, "What happens in _____ (*location*) stays in _____ (*location*)." We can forget how God spoke to us in the midst of our time here and go back to our lives as if nothing happened.

2. CONDEMN. We can get angry about the way our friends, families, and churches all seem stuck in their old ways and just don't seem to "get it."

3. CREATE. We can go home and find ways to get involved in kingdom service in our own backyards. We can choose to create a community that's centered on mission and that chooses to stay involved in righting wrongs so God's kingdom is made more clear.

Q: **In the past, how have you felt the temptations to consume or condemn after returning from a mission trip or maybe even a camp experience?**

Q: **Based on your past experiences, what would it take for us as a youth ministry to create a missional community at home?**

Distribute paper and pens and invite students to draw a line down the center of their paper. On the left side of their paper, ask students to draw a picture (or write words, phrases, or a poem) of how they have seen the "real" world of following Jesus this week. After students have finished that, ask them to draw (or write) something on the right side of the paper that captures how they'd like to live out the Jesus-focused "real world" when they get back home.

When students are finished, give them a chance to share their drawings. Notice any themes that emerge (e.g., sharing the gospel with our words, loving people who are poor, working hard to meet physical needs). For your time of closing prayer, invite students to gather in groups in different parts of the room around the theme that is most significant to them (e.g., "Anyone who wants to pray that we will be able to love those in our home community who are poor can meet by that back window").

HAVE MORE TIME?

In addition to praying along the themes that emerged from their drawings, invite students to get into working teams to tackle some of these issues at home. Give students time to brainstorm how they might be able to live out the "real world" they've seen in the midst of their service as they transition home. Invite each team to share some of their ideas and, if possible, schedule a time for those same teams to meet again within two or three weeks to check in and determine future action steps.

REVERSE CULTURE SHOCK

BY APRIL L. DIAZ

SOME SCRIPTURE

BIG IDEA: God doesn't want us to adjust to an earthly culture, but instead a kingdom culture.

You'll Need:

- Pictures from your trip. You may be able to display pictures for the entire group with a laptop, or you can ask students to bring their cameras and cell phones and simply flip through their pictures with teammates.
- Paper
- Pens
- Poster paper
- (Optional: Copies of the Romans 12:1-2 passage from *The Message* included in this exercise)

Welcome students and thank those who've agreed to share pictures from your recent justice work. Explain: **It's been said that a picture is worth ten thousand words, and I'm guessing that will be true with some of our pictures. I want you to take several minutes to flip through each other's pictures. As you do, please pay attention to any feelings or thoughts that occur to you.**

After students have finished looking at the pictures, distribute paper and pens. Ask students to draw a line down the center of their paper to create two columns. The left column should be labeled "during our justice work" and the right column should be labeled "at home." In the two columns, ask students to write descriptive words or phrases about the different aspects of the two cultures. To jar students' thinking you might want to write some prompts on poster paper, such as:

- Airports
- Markets / grocery stores
- Schools
- Restaurants
- Homes
- Churches

- Methods of transportation
- Roads
- Landscaping
- Shopping malls

Divide students into groups of three or four and have them discuss the following questions. (You can either print out copies of these questions in advance or read them one at a time, giving students a chance to discuss each question for a few minutes before you give the next question):

Q: **In what ways do the two cultures differ?**

Q: **What are some things the two cultures have in common?**

Q: **What are your feelings toward each of the cultures?**

Explain: **People who travel and experience a new culture often experience "reverse culture shock" when they return home, as elements of their home culture suddenly seem unfamiliar and even strange.**

Q: **What do you think you will struggle with the most in "reverse culture shock"?**

> Just as you and your students may have experienced culture shock when you began this trip, you may have even worse reverse culture shock as you reenter your home culture. As we return from such an intense time of justice work, we can easily become overwhelmed by the differences between the two cultures, especially the abundant resources of Western culture. (Even the number of toilet paper options at the grocery store can be traumatic.) This debrief will help you and your students articulate your emotions and discover how God desires for you to respond to different cultures.

At this point, lead your students in the practice *lectio divina* (pronounced LEK-tsea-oh dih-VEE-nuh), meaning "holy reading." *Lectio divina* is a method of prayerful reflection on a particular Scripture passage. In this case, we encourage you to ask students to reflect on this version of Romans 12:1-2 from *The Message*:

So here's what I want you to do, God helping you: Take your everyday, ordinary life—your sleeping, eating, going-to-work, and walking-around life—and place it before God as an offering. Embracing what God does for you is the best thing you can do for him. Don't become so well-adjusted to your culture that you fit into it without even thinking. Instead, fix your attention on God. You'll be changed from the inside out. Readily recognize what he wants from you, and quickly respond to it. Unlike the culture around you, always dragging you down to its level of immaturity, God brings the best out of you, develops well-formed maturity in you.

Begin by telling your students you are going to read a short passage from Scripture, and that you want to invite them to note any words or images that stand out to them. Then slowly read the passage above aloud to your students, savoring each phrase. (If you'd like, you can make copies of the passage ahead of time so students can follow along.) Then read the passage aloud, two more times, reminding them to listen for, and then reflect on, any particular words, phrases, images, or messages that emerge.

After a few minutes, invite students to pray silently, expressing whatever praises or petitions emerge from the way the Lord and this Romans passage are speaking to them.

Finally, allow students to rest silently before the Lord, experiencing his presence, love, and peace.

When you're finished, ask students to discuss the following with their small groups:

Q: **What images or experiences came to mind during this reading?**

Q: **What, if anything, did God say to you? Why do you think God is giving you this message?**

Q: **How can you apply that insight from Romans 12:1-2 to your reverse culture shock?**

Close by reading Romans 12:1-2 one final time, asking God to help your students fix their attention on him as you return to your home culture.

HAVE MORE TIME?

Daniel was a young man who experienced culture shock in transitioning from his Israelite culture to the Babylonian culture in the king's palace. He even had to change his name in order to live within that culture! Read Daniel 1:8-17 with your students to learn how Daniel and his friends dealt with the culture shock, and then discuss the following:

Q: **What things did Daniel and his friends do to stay separate from the culture while still remaining in it?**

Q: **What did Daniel do in response to the contrasting cultures?**

Q: **What did Daniel and his friends do to honor both God and the people in the culture at the same time?**

Q: **What can you do to be more like Daniel and his friends?**

BLESSING BEADS

BY KARA POWELL

BIG IDEA: Noticing the way each member of our team was a blessing as we served can help us continue to bless others once we're back home.

SOME
SCRIPTURE

You'll need:

- Each student will make a bracelet with thin leather rope and beads. The number of beads per bracelet should match the number of participants; so if you have 15 students in attendance, each of those students will need 15 beads, so you'll need to buy 225 beads. It's a good idea to have some extra beads handy also. Plus don't forget that thin leather rope. Ahead of time, cut one 10-inch segment of rope for each student (a few extras wouldn't hurt here, either) and place a piece of rope and the proper number of beads for each student in baggies for easy distribution later.

- (HAVE MORE TIME? option: Bibles)

Greet students and share a few of your own fresh memories of how the team worked together in the midst of serving others on your justice journey. Explain: **Each of you played an important part in the blessing we were to those we served, as well as to one another.**

Explain that we're going to take some time as a group to affirm ways each team member has blessed other people. Distribute the baggie with the rope and beads and ask the students to tie a knot in the end of the rope. Explain: **We're going to form a line** (or a circle if that fits your space better) **and each of us is going to hold a baggie of beads. We're going to walk through the line one at a time, and as we get to each person, that person is going to share how we were a blessing as we served—either to them personally or to others. After sharing those words of blessing, that person will put one of his beads on the rope we are holding. After we've all gone through the line, each of us should have one bead left over. Hold on to that last bead until later.**

At this point, pick the student at one end of the line to go first (we'll call her Student 1), and have her go to the first person (we'll call him Student 2—very creative) and hear how she was a blessing and receive a bead from him. Then Student 1 moves to Student 3, and so on. When Student 1 reaches the end of the line, she should assume the last position of the line and get ready to share how the next person coming down the line (Student 2), was a blessing. You can start Student 2 either when Student 1 is a few students ahead or you can wait until Student 1 is all the way through the line if you have the time and the desire for all your students to hear what everyone says.

HAVE MORE TIME?

Distribute Bibles to your students and turn to Acts 2:42-47 together. After you read the passage, lead the following discussion:

Q: **In what ways were people in this first-century church blessings to one another?**

Q: **How do these verses resemble the way we were blessings to one another as we served?**

Q: **What was the result of all these blessings in Acts 2:47?**

Q: **Who was it that was really drawing people to the early Christian community?**

Q: **How would you assess our resemblance to the Acts 2 church while we were together doing justice work? What makes it tough to be that kind of church back home?**

Q: **What goals might we set that would help us embody at home the same Acts 2 church spirit we experienced as we served?**

Why would Luke (the author of Acts) describe "the breaking of bread" in Acts 2:42 and then mention, just four verses later, that the believers "broke bread in their homes" (Acts 2:46)? Is he just being repetitious? Most scholars think that the use of the phrase "breaking of bread" in 2:42 refers to taking Communion, since it is lodged between phrases about fellowship and teaching. In contrast, 2:46 talks about eating "together with glad and sincere hearts," leading most theologians to conclude that this verse describes eating meals together.

Explain: **The rope and beads you're holding can remind you of how the Lord worked through you to bless others. But they can also be a reminder of another source of blessings—the blessings we received from the people in the community we served. I'd like you to take your final bead and, as you add it to your bracelet, please share aloud one way you were blessed by the people we served.**

Close by asking students to make a knot on the other end of their ropes so the beads won't roll off. Students can then tie the ends together to form a bracelet or key chain if they would like.

THE HOPE OF GLORY

BY BRAD GRIFFIN

BIG IDEA: When we hear others' perceptions of how Christ has been working in our lives, we are encouraged to embrace that transformation for ourselves.

SOME SCRIPTURE

You'll need:

- Index cards
- Bibles
- Paper
- Pens

After your justice work, set a time to bring closure to your students' experience of praying for one another by leading this activity and discussion. Open by asking:

> This exercise will work *way* better if you assigned prayer partners to your students during the trip as we suggested in our "heads up" note on page 86. But if not, no worries—it can still be effective. Simply modify the discussion accordingly and then assign students into pairs randomly when it's time to write letters.

Q: **Over the past few months each of us has been praying for another member of our team. What has that experience been like for you?**

Q: **Have you thought much about the fact that someone else is praying for *you*? What feelings has that sparked in you?**

Explain: **As we faithfully pray for one another, we are often changed in the process. Perhaps you've experienced that as you have been praying for your teammate. Perhaps you have also noticed change in the person you've been praying for during the course of our justice work. If you have had those sorts of experiences, would you feel comfortable sharing about them with us?**

Next read Colossians 1:24-29 to the group, or invite a student to read it. Point out that Paul is writing this letter from prison to a church in Colossae. Then ask:

Q: **What is the "mystery" Paul is talking about?** In verses 25-26 Paul describes it as "the word of God in its fullness," and in verse 27 he talks about the "glorious riches" of the mystery, "Christ in you, the hope of glory." Note also that Paul uses the word *mystery* in Colossians 2:2 and 4:3. Throughout Colossians it is Christ himself who is the mystery proclaimed.

Q: **What do you think Paul means by the "hope of glory"? What does it mean that we carry the hope of glory in us?** Note that one way to think about this phrase is to think about the hope we have in the final resurrection when Christ returns to bring the fullness of his kingdom (see Colossians 3:4). Another way to think about it is the glory of God that lives in us because of Christ's presence with us as believers.

Q: **How does our justice work reflect the "hope of glory"? What actions, attitudes, and values reflect the "hope of glory" in our lives at home?**

These verses from the first chapter of Colossians are part of one of the most important Christological passages in the New Testament. Colossians 1:15-20 is often referred to as one of the earliest hymns about Christ. Paul follows that hymn with some powerful statements about Jesus' identity and the reconciliation brought by his sacrifice on the cross (vv. 21-23). He goes on to call Christ the revelation of a mystery, "the word of God in its fullness" (v. 25). This mystery is made known not only to Jews, but also to Gentiles (and so to everyone, everywhere), as "Christ in you, the hope of glory." By making this statement, Paul boldly proclaims the power of Christ to *transform* us by dwelling *in* us. As he does, our lives proclaim the gospel of hope to others.

Now think again about the person you've been praying for. Think about Christ in that person, the hope of glory. Remember back over the course of our time in the midst of our justice work, and recall ways that person has impacted others—both within our team and outside it.

Today we are each going to write a letter to that teammate we have been praying for. In your letter, share about how you have seen that person grow, and how that individual has contributed to the team's growth and to the lives of the locals where we served.

We're going to focus our reflection through this one phrase from Scripture, which I'd like you to write at the top of the letter: "Christ in you, the hope of glory."

Allow students time to write their letters, perhaps playing music in the background or sending them out to reflect and write alone and then gather back together. Invite students to share their letters with each other and to pray for each other. If you have time, close this meeting with a meal or snacks to celebrate Christ in you (plural), the hope of glory!

WHO'S MY NEIGHBOR?

BY DAVE LIVERMORE

BIG IDEA: We can share with people in our own schools and community the same love for others we lived out during our justice journey.

LOTSA SCRIPTURE

You'll need:

- Copies of your local newspaper
- Pens
- Paper or copies of the *Deep Justice Journeys Student Journal* (pages 121-123)
- Bibles
- (HAVE MORE TIME? option: Drivers and permission to take your students on a brief "tour")

Greet your students and invite them to share a few brief stories about some of their favorite people they met during your recent justice work. Then distribute local newspapers from your community and ask them to share any initial thoughts or feelings as they thumb through images of their home community.

> The road from Jerusalem to Jericho was about 17 miles long and curved through rugged terrain with plenty of large rocks for thieves to hide behind. As a result, traveling this road was very dangerous.

Acknowledge that flying off to serve Hondurans or spending time doing service in a very different community here in the United States can be an exhilarating experience. It's easy to fall in love with people for a few days in the midst of the excitement of justice work.

Continue: **Coming back home to the people in our own neighborhoods isn't quite as exciting or glamorous. But we don't primarily live out the gospel in faraway places a couple of weeks a year. We live out the gospel 24/7 with the people at school, at home, and in the neighborhood.**

Transition to one of Jesus' most popular stories—the parable of the good Samaritan—by giving students some background: Jesus tells the story of the good Samaritan right after he's said that loving God and loving your neighbor are the most important commandments. An obvious application would be to see that loving your neighbor means helping the person in need along the roadside, at the lunch table, or in Sudan. At this point, invite a few students to read Luke 10:25-37 aloud.

Q: **In Luke 10:27, Jesus teaches we are to love God and love our neighbor. How, if at all, are those two love commands connected to each other?**

Q: **How does Jesus define a "neighbor"?**

Q: **Based on Jesus' definition, who are your "neighbors"?**

Q: **What would it mean for you to love them as yourself?**

HAVE MORE TIME?

Ask your students to get into small groups to come up with a modern-day version of this parable set in their own school(s) or your city. Once the small groups are finished developing their contemporary versions of Jesus' parable, have them act them out for the rest of the group.

Continue: **It's possible that your justice journey gave you new opportunities to interact with people whose racial or ethnic background is different from your own. It's worth considering how Jesus' story of the good Samaritan speaks to issues of racism and racial stereotyping. Racism and stereotyping are not new problems. During Jesus' lifetime, both were widespread. For example, most first-century Jews couldn't stand Samaritans. So when Jesus uses a Samaritan as the role model for living out the greatest commandments, instead of the priest or Levite, his Jewish audience must have been shocked!**

So Jesus not only calls the Jews to watch out for the wounded and oppressed alongside the road; he also invites the Jews to love the Samaritans and to realize they as Jews have something to learn from the Samaritans.

Have students respond to the following on a piece of paper. Tell them no one else will read this:

Q: **Who are the "Samaritans" in your life—the people who seem so different that you find it hard to relate to them? Are there certain groups or individuals who make you annoyed or anxious because they feel unfamiliar to you?**

After your students have had some time to reflect on these questions, ask them to respond in writing to this question: **What would it look like for you to love those neighbor(s) as you love yourself this week?**

After students have finished writing their answers to that question, invite them to write down their answers to the following: **What impact would loving those people as you love yourself have on the way you love God?**

After students have finished, invite them to form a circle to close in prayer. They will likely choose to face the center of the circle. Point out that our tendency is to face inward, but that Jesus' words in Luke 10 invite us to face outward. So ask your students to turn around and face outward as a sign of their desire to be open to new relationships with people who feel different from ourselves. Invite a few students to close by praying aloud that God would help us love him with our hearts, souls, and strength, and also give us the strength to love our neighbors as ourselves.

HAVE MORE TIME?

To help your students see how they can love their neighbors all day long, during this exercise or at some point in the future travel together to a few of the places where they spend time (school, home, coffee shop, mall, a workplace). At each place talk about some of the people there. Push them beyond superficial responses and ask questions like:

Q: **What's it like to be here?**

Q: **With whom do you typically interact when you're here?**

Q: **Who is hardest for you to love here? Why?**

Q: **What if this were a short-term mission trip destination instead? How would that cause you to view the people here?**

AFTER: ONGOING TRANSFORMATION

Connecting the dots between your justice work and daily life for the next several weeks and months…

REENTRY

BY TODD BRATULICH

NO SCRIPTURE

BIG IDEA: Returning from a short-term mission trip can be difficult and disorienting, but it does not have to paralyze us. We can live differently as a result of our experience!

You'll need:

- Five sheets of poster paper, hung in different sections of your meeting space
- Markers
- Paper
- Pens or pencils

Begin by greeting everyone: **Welcome back. It's great to be back together as a team after justice work. Today we want to talk about what it feels like to be back home. Most of us probably have some mixed emotions about what we've experienced and how our past justice work relates to our life at home now. I want to reassure you this is normal. Let's begin by discussing two questions together.**

Get into a circle (or break up into smaller groups if your group is large) and invite each student to answer the following two questions:

Q: **What has been the hardest part about being back home?**

Q: **What has been the best part about being back home?**

Continue: **Does anyone remember February 1, 2003? That was the day when the U.S. space shuttle named *Columbia* disintegrated over Texas during its reentry into the earth's atmosphere. That day should have brought celebration—the mission had been a success, new insights had been gained through research, and the crew of seven astronauts were on their way back home. But due to a damaged thermal tile on the shuttle's exterior, the shuttle burst into flames as it reentered the atmosphere and all seven crew members died.**

Reentry into life back home after a mission trip can sometimes leave us burnt and broken up as well. We come home feeling that God has changed us, and we want to live differently because of it. But it can be difficult to figure out how to do that as we enter back into our own culture and old habits.

In the *Short-Term Missions Workbook*, **Tim Dearborn describes four common experiences for people returning from a cross-cultural mission experience:**[22]

1. **Fun: We like returning to the comforts we enjoy back home.**

2. **Flee: We miss our team and struggle to find people we can share our experience with, so we end up feeling lonely and isolated.**

3. **Fight: We get frustrated with our own culture's selfishness or indifference and fight against conforming to it.**

4. **Fit: We grow tired of fighting and just try to fit back into our own culture.**

Take four sheets of poster paper, and write one of the four common reactions to returning home from cross-cultural mission experiences (FUN, FLEE, FIGHT, FIT) as a header at the top of each one. (Leave the fifth sheet blank; we'll come back to that later). Under each header, write one related question that will prompt your group to deeper reflection. Some possible questions are:

- Fun: What was the most fun or pleasurable comfort to return home to?

- Flee: When have you felt lonely or isolated since you've been back? With whom has it been difficult for you to share your experience?

- Fight: What do you dislike about the culture you've come home to?

- Fit: What old habits have you returned to since you've been back? What new habits or commitments have been most difficult to follow since you've returned?

Give every student a marker and invite all of them to walk around the room and write their own answers to the questions on each sheet. Once students have finished, gather the posters and share some of the responses with the group. With each poster, invite discussion by asking a few of the following questions:

Q: **Would anyone like to share what you wrote about this response and explain why you wrote it?**

Q: **What are a few ways we could work through this response/emotion in a healthy manner?**

Q: **Why do you think it is important to pay attention to these responses and emotions?**

Explain: **Again, I want to encourage you and let you know all of these reactions are normal and okay. The important thing is that we press on and recognize they are all part of God's ongoing transformation in our lives. We don't often change overnight; it usually takes hard work and a lot of dependence upon the Lord to process what we've experienced and let it really transform how we think, relate, and live from now on.**

At this point, turn to the remaining sheet of poster paper and invite students to share words or images that describe how they would like to be responding to their reentry to life at home. If your students are able to arrive at a consensus of a few terms or images that best reflect your group's intentions, that's all the better.

---

22. Adapted from Tim Dearborn, *Short-Term Missions Workbook: From Mission Tourist to Global Citizen* (Downers Grove: InterVarsity Press, 2003), 94-96.

Close by distributing paper to the students and inviting each of them to write a prayer letter to God. Invite them to begin their letter by writing, "Dear God..." From there, encourage students to write to God about ways their own lives have matched one or more of the responses (Fun, Flee, Fight, Fit) as well as how they feel about that. Prompt them to confess any sinfulness they see in themselves in the midst of the transition home, and encourage them to ask God to give them grace to be the kingdom people he wants them to be.

Suggestions for Overcoming a Rough Reentry:[23]

Write about it! Journaling helps you sort through your thoughts and feelings and allows you to express them in a healthy way.

Talk about it! Find two people you trust, and share your experience with them. Tell them your stories, your hopes, your frustrations—tell them everything—and ask them to pray for you as you translate your justice experience into your life back home. (For more hints on how to do that, see "Shaped by Mentors" on page 159).

Do something about it! Identify an issue or a need in your own community and do something to address it. If you are concerned with poverty, find out who is working to help impoverished people in your community and volunteer to serve with them.

Embrace it! Incorporating into your everyday life and faith what you have experienced on your mission trip is an ongoing process. It's okay to have doubts, questions, and mixed emotions. Remember that every step of the journey is important, no matter how small.

---

23. Dearborn, 94-96.

SHAPED BY MENTORS

BY KARA POWELL AND BRAD GRIFFIN

BIG IDEA: God shapes us in many ways, including through the wisdom of our adult mentors.

SOME
SCRIPTURE

You'll need:

- To plan a sharing meeting that includes students' parents and mentors. Ideally, you'd ask each student who served to choose a mentor. If you chose to do the "Mentoring for Justice" exercise on page 40, it would be logical (but not mandatory) for students to have the same people serve as mentors both BEFORE and AFTER the justice work. Once you schedule the sharing meeting, it would be wise to design an invitation you can e-mail to your students that they can forward to their parents and mentors. If your students have been working through the *Deep Justice Journeys Student Journal,* encourage them to bring their journals with them as catalysts for their sharing. Ask mentors to bring their Bibles. Make it clear in your invitation that students should attend the meeting even if they are unable to bring their parents or mentors. You (plus maybe other adult volunteers if needed) can play the mentoring role in the meeting.

- To set the tone for your sharing by creating as warm and intimate an environment as possible. Adjust the lighting, light some candles, and serve drinks and treats.

- Copies of the **Before/During/After Model** handout (page 15)

- Copies of the **Mentoring for Justice: Questions for Students and Mentors AFTER Our Justice Work** handout (page 161)

- Clay or Play-Doh for each student

- Small baggies

- Bibles

To begin your sharing meeting, welcome students and their parents and mentors. Set a friendly tone by sharing a few ways your recent justice work impacted you personally.

Distribute the copies of the **Before/During/After Model** handout to the group and give a brief explanation of all the stages. (You'll find some helpful talking points about the model in the "Initial Steps" chapter on pages 9-11. The handout itself is at the end of that same chapter on page 15). Point out that for many teenagers who serve, most of what impacted them fades away once they get home. Research indicates that one factor that can bolster students' long-term growth is having multiple adults support them as they connect the dots between their justice work and their lives at home.

At this point, ask your students to introduce themselves as well as the adults who have come with them. If your group is small enough and/or trusting enough, ask your students to share why they invited these particular mentor(s) by describing what they respect about them.

If you have a media presentation that captures your justice work (video, Power Point presentation, slide show, etc.), this is a good time to play it.

Transition into a time of sharing by giving some clay or Play-Doh to each student. Invite them to play with the clay in their hands as you explain that our lives are like this clay, and that hopefully God has been shaping them through the recent justice mission. Read aloud Isaiah 64:8, which teaches, "Yet you, LORD, are our Father. We are the clay, you are the potter; we are all the work of your hand."

> The same imagery of God's potter-ness and our clay-ness is also used by Paul in Romans 9:19-21.

Then give an opportunity for students to share with their mentors and parents one or more *specific* ways the justice work shaped them. You can either do this together as a large group, or ask students to gather with their parents and/or mentors to share individually. If students have brought their journals, encourage them to read aloud any excerpts that seem especially relevant or poignant.

After students have had time to share, explain: **Now that the mentors and parents have heard from their students, it's time for those wise adults to speak into our lives. My hope is that the adults you've invited will have one or more Scripture verses or other insights that relate to what you've shared that can help you continue to be molded and shaped by the Lord.** Give plenty of time for adults to share with students, and for students and adults to ask one another questions. Make sure you're available to meet with students who were unable to have other adults with them.

When the sharing has concluded, ask students to divide the clay you've given them so every adult they've invited also gets a chunk of clay. Close in prayer together as every person in the room holds a piece of clay. Invite the adults to pray aloud that the Lord would continue the good work in these students as they face temptations and distractions now that they are back at home.

Before everyone leaves, distribute plastic bags to everyone so they can take the clay home with them. Also, ask students to talk with their mentors before they walk out the door about whether they'd like to meet again on their own, or have a phone call in a few weeks to share more about how the Lord continues to shape them. Feel free to distribute copies of the **Mentoring for Justice: Questions for Students and Mentors AFTER Our Justice Work** handout as future conversation-starters for adults and students.

QUESTIONS FOR STUDENTS AND MENTORS
AFTER OUR JUSTICE WORK

1. What one word or phrase would you use to describe your experience?

2. If you could add a few more words or phrases to more fully describe your experience, what would they be?

3. What surprised you? How did that impact your justice work?

4. What disappointed you? What do you wish had been different about your experience? How did that impact your justice work?

5. When were you most overwhelmed? What did you do about that, or how did you respond to that feeling?

6. How was life in the place you visited different than you thought it would be? What discoveries did you make?

7. Where did you sense God at work in your life and in the lives of others during this justice mission?

8. What do you think other people saw in you during your time serving?

9. What has it been like to reenter life with your family and friends at home? What kinds of feelings are you experiencing?

10. How do you see life here differently now? How do you feel about that? Where do you sense God at work here?

11. What do you hope will change about your life as a result of this experience? Who can help you make those changes or hold you accountable for them?

12. How should our church change as a result of your team's experience?

13. How can you live out justice beyond this particular experience? What dreams do you have for justice both where you visited and here at home?

14. How are you going to talk with others about your justice work? If you were going to share a 30-second version of your experience, what would you say?

PAYING ATTENTION TO THE PRESENCE OF GOD

BY TODD BRATULICH

LOTSA SCRIPTURE

BIG IDEA: Practicing spiritual disciplines helps us experience God's presence and notice God's activity in our lives after we return from our justice work.

You'll need:

- Clip from the movie *Bruce Almighty* in which Bruce is asking for an answer or sign from God. Clip begins at 21:00 into the movie and ends at 25:16.

- Bibles

- Poster paper or a whiteboard

- Copies of the **Practicing the Disciplines** handout (pages 165-166), and/or copies of the *Deep Justice Journeys Student Journal* (pages 129-131)

Welcome your students and set up the video clip by sharing that Bruce, played by Jim Carrey, has had everything seem to go wrong all at once. He just lost his job, got beat up trying to help someone out, and had a tough argument with his wife. Now, he is out for a drive, questioning God and trying to make sense of his life. Play the four-minute clip and then lead the following discussion:

Q: **How did Bruce try to get God's attention? How did that work?**

Q: **How did God try to get Bruce's attention? Did it work? Why or why not?**

Q: **Have you ever felt like Bruce, looking for God's presence and not finding it? How did you seek God in the midst of those times?**

Continue: **Sometimes after we come back from doing justice work, we can feel like God's presence seems to disappear. When we were serving, we experienced God's presence so intensely. But when we get home, we may find it difficult to feel that same sense of intimacy with God.**

Q: **Why do you think people often feel God's presence so intensely on mission trips?**

Q: **What was your most memorable time of sensing God's presence during your service work?**

Q: **Why do you think it is so much more difficult to experience God's presence once you've returned home?**

Continue: **The reality is that God is always present with us, but like Bruce in the movie, we often miss God. We pay so much attention to our own desires, needs, and concerns that we are often oblivious to the small ways God is speaking to us or working in our lives. Experiencing God's presence beyond our justice work can happen when we pay attention to what God is doing in and around us. But let's be honest: We live in a noisy world in which paying attention is hard work and takes discipline.**

Divide your students into groups of no more than five people. Give each group one of the following passages. Give students time to look up and read the passage together and answer the three questions that follow. Write the three questions on a whiteboard or poster paper so students can refer back to them.

Scripture Passages:

1. Numbers 22 (the entire chapter or just verses 21-41 if time is short) – Balaam's donkey
2. Daniel 3:8-30 – Shadrach, Meshach, and Abednego
3. Luke 24:13-35 – Jesus on the road to Emmaus
4. Matthew 14:22-33 – Jesus invites Peter to walk on the water

Small-Group Questions:

1. **How was God at work in your story? What was God doing among the people?**
2. **How did the people in this story pay attention to God? How did they not pay attention to God?**
3. **What happened when God got their attention? How did it change their perspectives?**

Bring the entire group back together and invite each small group to share what they learned from their story about paying attention to God.

Explain: **Even the Israelite prophets and the people closest to Jesus often had a hard time paying attention to God. Like us, they were easily distracted by all the voices and activity that surrounded them. Fortunately, in the midst of our distractions, God has shown us—through Jesus, through people in the Bible, and through the saints throughout history—that we can learn to pay attention to God's presence and God's activity in our lives. But like any other discipline, it takes practice to pay attention to God.**

My hunch is we can even learn from one another and the different ways each of us experiences God's presence. What are some of the ways you tend to connect with God?

At this point, distribute copies of the **Practicing the Disciplines** handout and let students respond to its questions. After students have finished, have them share their answers either in small groups or with your entire group. Close by practicing one of the disciplines listed—prayer—with your students, asking God to help you all experience his presence in new and meaningful ways in the days to come.

HAVE MORE TIME?

Invite students to do some additional homework on a spiritual discipline. Challenge them to research one of the classic spiritual disciplines online or refer them to some of the following resources. Then invite them to practice for a week the spiritual discipline they've chosen and report back to the group about their experiences at your next meeting:

- Foster, Richard, *Celebration of Discipline*, San Francisco: HarperCollins, 1978. This is a classic one-volume text on spiritual disciplines. It might be a little heavy for teenagers, but it's a great resource for youth workers.

- Jones, Tony, *Soul Shaper*, Grand Rapids: Zondervan, 2003. This book is a great guide to exploring contemplative practices in youth ministry.

- Robbins, Duffy and Maggie, *Enjoy the Silence: A 30 Day Experiment in Listening to God*, Grand Rapids: Zondervan, 2006. This 30-day devotional journey leads students toward a posture of listening to God through the practice of *lectio divina*.

If time permits, you could print information from websites ahead of time about these disciplines and/or have copies of the books listed above for students to peruse in the midst of your group meeting.

PRACTICING THE DISCIPLINES

▶ PAGE 1 ◀

Read through the list of classic spiritual disciplines below. Underline any that you've practiced or participated in before. Circle one or two that you have never experienced, but would like to try.

MEDITATION: The discipline of slowing down and cutting out all the noise around you so you can focus your heart and mind on Jesus Christ. It might include imagining yourself with Jesus or just thinking about God's love.

PRAYER: The practice of listening to and talking with God, not just when you fold your hands and close your eyes, but any and every time you communicate or simply commune with God.

STUDY: The discipline of searching for the truth of God through the Scriptures, creation, church tradition, and the wisdom of saints who have gone before you.

FASTING: The discipline of abstaining from something and being filled instead by the presence of God. It could include abstaining from food, your iPod, grande mocha frappuccinos, or anything else you use for fulfillment.

SIMPLICITY: The discipline of living without being enslaved to your stuff (cars, clothes, gadgets, bling, etc...). Simplicity is about being free from the control of materialism so you can freely give to and receive from others.

SOLITUDE: The practice of being alone and facing your loneliness as you encounter God. Solitude allows you to face yourself and come face-to-face with God without the comfort or distraction of others.

SUBMISSION: The discipline of denying yourself, often to give to another, not out of duty but in love and freedom. It can include giving up your power, possessions, comfort, opinions, and even your life for the sake of others.

SERVICE: The act of humbling yourself and serving the needs of others. Jesus modeled this discipline in washing his disciples' feet.

CONFESSION: The discipline of confessing your sins and temptations to a trusted believer. In confession, you are able to forgive and bear with another as you experience God's grace and forgiveness.

WORSHIP: The practice of acknowledging God's presence and responding to God's grace, beauty, and love. Worship can be expressed in silence, in song, even in creating art or playing in God's creation.

GUIDANCE: The act of seeking the wisdom of others for direction in your life and spiritual journey. It involves seeking the guidance of the Holy Spirit through the voice of a faithful community (trusted friends and family who love and follow God, youth group, pastors or mentors, etc...).

CELEBRATION: The practice of partying! Remember, the gospel literally means "good news!" You have every reason to celebrate God's goodness, enjoy God's creation, and embrace the people God has put in your life.

The descriptions of the disciplines are adapted from Richard Foster's *Celebration of Discipline* (San Francisco: HarperCollins, 1978).

▶ PAGE 2 ◀

Now, look back at the spiritual discipline(s) you underlined. What can you do this week to experience God's presence through practicing one or more of these disciplines in a fresh and new way?

Look at the spiritual discipline(s) you circled. How will you explore those disciplines this week?

Whom will you ask to practice this new spiritual discipline(s) with you—or to hold you accountable as you practice it?

LENSES FOR THE FUTURE

BY BRAD GRIFFIN

NO SCRIPTURE

BIG IDEA: After our justice work, it's important to spend some time dreaming for the future together, imagining what the "next chapter" might look like in our corporate story of faith.

You'll need:

- Photos or video you've taken of five to ten everyday household objects (e.g., toothbrush, cell phone, screwdriver) or objects from around your youth room or church. Start with a very blurry (and perhaps too-close) shot, and then take a well-focused shot (or focus your video camera by slowly zooming out). Prepare these for viewing by students in some way (television or projector) for the opening exercise.

- A piece of paper for each team to use in the opening exercise

- Pens or pencils

- Three index cards for each student (it's a good idea to have extras, too)

- Tape

- Four large sheets of poster paper on the walls, with one of the following labels on each one: TODAY, NEXT MONTH, NEXT YEAR, and ACTION STEPS. Ahead of time, tape the four pieces of poster paper to different walls in your meeting space.

Open by saying: **We're going to start by looking at some everyday items. In teams of three, please discuss and then write down what each object is as we go through the pictures.** Distribute paper and a pen or pencil to each group. Depending on how many objects you've photographed or videoed, have each team make a numbered list and write their guesses by each number as you first show them the blurry objects. Then show them the clear images, and see which team had the most right answers. (If you use video, you will want to pause it each time to let them write down their guesses before letting the camera refocus.) Give the winning team a special privilege, like going first in line at your next meal or getting some kind of treat. Then debrief by asking:

Q: **Was it easy for you to figure out what the items were at first? Why or why not?**

Q: **What kinds of feelings did you experience while we played this game?** Students might share that they felt frustrated, cheated, or helpless. Some might have given up, thought it was fun, or been too apathetic to even try.

Q: Thinking back to our recent justice work, did you experience any of those same emotions?

Q: In what ways was our justice work similar to looking through a camera that's *out* of focus? In what ways was the experience like looking through a camera that's *in* focus?

Q: How many of you would say you have a clearer picture of life in our host community now than before our justice work? Why do you think that?

Q: How many would say you have a clearer picture of life back home now than before our service? Why is that?

Q: Would anyone say the opposite? That you had a clearer picture of home or our host community before our justice work—but now it seems fuzzier?

Continue by sharing: **Sometimes it can seem like life gets out of focus and we can't tell what we're looking at anymore. Doing justice work can lead to those kinds of feelings because over a short period of time we're given new lenses through which we must look at the world in a different way. Coming home can make those feelings even more confusing, because suddenly we look at our lives back home in a different way, too.**

Sometimes when we zoom out and refocus—or perhaps reframe the shot altogether—we see life more clearly. Sometimes we discover that we see God more clearly, too. Perhaps in the midst of our justice work, God has given you new lenses to see in new ways our life together and our hopes for the future.

Q: What are some ways you see life differently now than before our justice work?

Q: When you think about the future of our youth ministry, how do you see things differently now? What do you like about what you see, and what concerns or disturbs you?

After students share some of these insights, continue by saying: **Next we're going to do some dreaming together about our future. In light of all we've seen and experienced, and in light of the new lenses we've been given, we are going to zoom out, reframe our shot, and focus in on where God might be leading us together.**

Pause to take some time to pray about this before moving on, thanking God for giving us new ways to see, and inviting God to speak into the vision you collectively develop for the future.

Next distribute three index cards and pens or pencils to each person and have students get back into their groups of three. Point to the three sheets of paper taped around the room labeled TODAY, NEXT MONTH, and NEXT YEAR and say: **Now we are going to write a story. It's our story—and while we know this story has been going on for a while, what I'd like us to do now is dream together about the next chapter. I'd like for you to imagine this chapter in terms of three time periods: "today"—right now and the immediate future; "next month"—looking ahead a month or more; and "next year"—thinking at least a year out and further.**

When authors write books, sometimes they use storyboards to help them brainstorm ideas and see their thoughts on paper—or maybe even on the walls. Today we are going to make these sheets our storyboard for writing our next chapter together.

With your small group of three, talk together for a few minutes about each of these three categories. The main question I'd like for you to think about is this: **What dreams do you think God has for those time periods, in light of what we've just experienced through our justice work?** You might want to write that "main question" on a whiteboard or a different sheet of poster paper so students can remember it. **Brainstorm ideas and dreams for what God might want to do given all we've seen, experienced, and learned recently. Think locally as well as globally in your dreaming. On your index cards, I'd like for you to write down some of your ideas and dreams. You have three cards each, so as a group you can contribute three cards to each timeframe on the wall. After you have written your ideas, tape them to the appropriate part of our story. Remember that there are no bad ideas when we're brainstorming—don't be afraid to write something even if it seems a bit wild. In fact, the wilder, the better.**

See "Your Kingdom Come" on page 119 for more ideas about praying the Lord's Prayer together.

Give students plenty of time to brainstorm and contribute to the storyboard. Then gather everyone back and read the ideas on each section of the storyboard, stopping after each category (today, next month, and next year) to ask:

Q: **What are your initial thoughts about these ideas and dreams? What themes did you hear as we read through them? What other ideas does that spark?** Be sure to have someone write down those ideas on extra index cards and tape them to the storyboard.

After you've gone through all three storyboard sheets, ask:

Q: **What are some action steps we need to take based on what we've just written together? Who will be involved in taking those steps?** Have someone write your ideas up on the "Action Steps" sheet, keeping them as clear and action-oriented as possible. (Hint: Each step should have an active verb and a tangible outcome, and should be no more than one sentence.)

Close your discussion by saying: **One privilege of being part of God's kingdom ministry is that we get to participate in writing the story alongside God. This is a bit of a mystery; of course, God is in charge and knows the big picture, but at the same time he lets us all play a part along the way. Today we have written some God-sized dreams on the walls. Now let's pray that God will help us focus on and follow the ones that lead to God's will being done.**

This storyboard lends itself to a number of possibilities. You might invite student artists to paint images of your next chapter to display on the walls. Or you may have a creative writer in your group who can take down the cards and write a narrative using the ideas generated during your brainstorming. (This narrative could be used to help your leadership think through the next steps your ministry may want to take toward seeing God's justice done on earth "as it is in heaven.")

Additionally, you may want to leave these storyboard sheets on your wall for the next month or so, then gather the team again to review your dreams and perhaps revise them based on how you have (or haven't) been living them out. Perhaps you'll want to create a new storyboard, or commit to writing a new storyboard together in another couple of months.

Conclude your time in prayer, perhaps having students break out into groups of three again and inviting each person to pray for one of the three different areas on the storyboard. Or you might want to have students pray silently, inviting them to come write their names by action steps to signal their commitment to help take that particular step forward. Pray that your dreams would be kingdom dreams, and that as a group you would pursue God's will. Close by saying the Lord's Prayer together.

A COMMUNAL RULE OF LIFE

BY KURT RIETEMA

LOTSA SCRIPTURE

BIG IDEA: When your entire group gathers to celebrate a successful mission experience, students who participated in the trip as well as those who did not can join together to move the group in a kingdom direction.

You'll need:

- Bibles

- Food indigenous to the location in which you served. If possible, ask some of your students and/or their parents to provide the food so they feel ownership for the discussion (and so you can focus your time and energy on something else).

- (HAVE MORE TIME? option: Supplies for a mural or collage)

Students who didn't get to participate in your justice work for one reason or another are always in danger of feeling isolated from those who went. Inside jokes and stories only add to the frustration they sometimes feel. This exercise gets ALL your students involved in the bigger story of how God is moving you forward as a community. This exercise can help students remember that those who didn't participate in your recent justice work are just as important to the group as those who did. So please do this ongoing transformation exercise with your entire youth ministry.

Begin by sharing a story of a time when you felt left out. It's best if the story is from your own adolescence. (Most of us have a whole closet full of stories of teenage rejection!)

Q: **I've got a question for those of you who went on our justice trip: How do you think those who didn't go might be feeling? In what ways might they feel like they missed out?**

Continue: **The reality is that those who didn't go might have missed this trip but they are an important part of God's ongoing work in our midst. There's an Old Testament story in Numbers 13 that helps me understand the impact a small team of folks can have on a whole group. Under Moses' leadership the Israelites had left Egypt and were traveling (and often wandering) in the desert on their way to the Promised Land. Before God sent Israel into the Promised Land, Moses sent a group of 12 men to do some reconnaissance work, asking them to report back to the rest of the Israelites what they saw and experienced.** Read Numbers 13:17-20 aloud to give a sense of the type of questions Moses hoped the 12 men would investigate.

Now read Numbers 13:26-29 and 13:31-32 aloud so students can hear the report of the men when they returned.

Continue: **But not all 12 members of the team felt this way. Two men had a different report.** At this point, read Numbers 13:30 and 14:5-9.

Even though most of the men doubted God would provide the land, all 12 agreed on one thing: They all thought the land was great (Numbers 13:27). Some of you who participated in our recent justice work also got a taste of something great when you saw God's kingdom and the church in action. Can a few of you please share what you experienced?

Q: **Why do you think God told Moses to send a small group of explorers to go check out the land? What was their responsibility toward the rest of Israel?**

Explain: **The group of explorers failed. They saw what God had intended to give to Israel, but the majority of them never believed they could have it because they doubted God would protect and guide them. Israel should have listened to Joshua and Caleb because those two men truly wanted what God had in store for them and believed that God would provide it.**

So now let's switch the focus to our group. One reason we sent this group of students on a service trip was that we hoped they'd have an opportunity to serve God and see his kingdom in ways that would deepen their own faith. But it's also our hope that through them—their stories, their experiences, and the people they met and served—God will bring us ALL to a new place. We hope we'll ALL be compelled to change. We hope we will be a different youth group and a different church.

But we can't make these changes alone, and we can't make them on our own strength. Most of us probably have long lists of failed New Year's resolutions, or promises we made to God at camp and during mission trips, that we didn't live up to. The only way we can succeed is together with the power of the Holy Spirit.

Today, we're going to have a feast—literally—from the Promised Land that some of us just visited. We're going to share some food we ate there, and as we do, we'll share more about the experiences that gave us a glimpse of the kingdom and the God who protects and guides us. As we eat, those of you who didn't go on the justice trip can dream with us about how God wants us ALL to move forward.

At this point, serve authentic food from the place you visited—whether it's Mexican, Chinese, soul food, or macaroni and cheese. If you have time, invite students who went on your justice trip to share stories, videos, or photos of what they experienced, as well as dreams they have for your ministry here at home.

Q: **Those of you who didn't go on this trip, what themes did you hear from the stories and dreams?**

Q: **How do those themes relate to your own dreams for our ministry and community here?**

Explain: **Today we are going to create a common "rule of life," which is an ancient practice among many Christian communities. In his book,** *The Sacred Way,* **Tony Jones describes a rule of life as "a pattern of spiritual disciplines that provides structure and direction for growth in holiness."[24] Basically, adopting a common "rule of life" means that we choose together a few things we want to do regularly that help us become the kind of community God desires. And once we successfully incorporate those into our lives, we might adopt new ones.**

---

24. Tony Jones, *The Sacred Way* (Grand Rapids: Zondervan, 2005), 197.

Thinking back to some of your dreams for this community, what might be a few things you'd like to see as part of our rule of life? Let's see how many ideas we can come up with...

It is much better for students to come up with these ideas on their own at a grassroots level rather than having them imposed from the top down (meaning by you). If they are having difficulty, help them recall how they saw the kingdom of God in the midst of their justice work and how they might begin to create similar opportunities to see God's kingdom back at home. Here are some suggestions:

- Spend at least a few nights each week at home with our families, not watching television and not in our rooms.

- Twice a week, sit with someone in the lunchroom who doesn't seem to have many other friends.

- Develop a plan for Bible reading or morning and evening prayers everyone in the youth group commits to practicing four times per week.

- Commit together to the goal of giving a certain percentage of your income away to mission and justice efforts.

- Commit to fasting one day a week from "excessive" or self-focused purchases like snacks, candy, CDs, or music downloads.

- Participate in a mission trip every other year and, in the years you don't take a trip, help support ongoing, indigenous efforts at justice, development, and mission, using the money you'd have spent.

- If you traveled internationally, spend time once a month with local populations from that country. As a youth group, regularly go to church services, restaurants, or neighborhoods of that ethnic group.

After students are finished brainstorming, give each student four votes and ask them to vote for the practices they think will make the most difference in your ministry. After you've identified the four practices your group will take on, have your students begin to make them specific rather than open-ended (e.g., What are we going to read together? How often? Whom are we going to serve? When will that happen? Who is going to lead us in doing that?). Once you have four specific practices, decide which two or three you will start immediately. The hope is that after your group becomes faithful with those two or three, you can begin to add another practice(s) into your rhythm.

After you have come up with the two or three specific practices, ask how you can keep each other accountable to the rule and how you can share about what you've experienced together. Remind students that a rule of life is a way to grow in our experience of grace, not a legalistic set of absolutes.

Close in prayer in groups of three to five students, making sure each group comprises students who went on your recent justice trip as well as those who didn't. Encourage students to pray for one another as well as for God's ongoing work in your youth ministry, your church, and your community.

HAVE MORE TIME?

Have your students make a collage or painting to put in the youth room as a visual reminder of what kind of community you'd like to be. If possible, highlight the two or three practices you've chosen as part of the collage.

A PICTURE'S WORTH A LOT OF WORDS

BY KARA POWELL

BIG IDEA: There are more connections between our justice work and our lives at home than we might realize.

NO SCRIPTURE

You'll need:

- Pictures from your justice experience (make them at least 5 x 7 if not 8 x 10). You want more pictures than students, so if you expect 12 students at your meeting, print 18 to 24 pictures.
- Similarly, print pictures of various scenes that represent your students' lives at home. These might include a nearby shopping mall, a typical house in your town, a high school, a movie theatre, or a coffee shop. You might even ask a few students to be the shutterbugs and take and/or print out these pictures.

Welcome students and then ask: **Think back to our justice work and imagine that your mind is a camera. What images and memories of our experience are most vivid?**

Display pictures of your time serving along a table or a wall. Ask your students to come and look at the pictures without talking. After a few minutes, invite each student to choose a picture that triggers a significant thought or feeling. If more than one student wants the same picture, that's okay; they can both work from the same picture.

Divide your students into groups of three or four and explain: **I'd like each group member to share about the picture he or she chose and why it's personally significant. After each person has shared, the rest of the group can add comments or insights about that picture or the person who shares it, based on what they remember from our justice work.**

After the groups have finished, display the pictures of life at home in the same way. Again ask students to come and look at the pictures without talking, and then choose one picture that's significant to them.

Invite the students to return to their small groups and share about the pictures they've chosen and why they are significant. Similar to before, the rest of the group should add comments or insights about that picture or the person who has just shared.

After the small groups have finished, explain: **There's one more question I'd like us to discuss. You've talked about the picture from our trip, and you've talked about the home picture. But you haven't talked about how the two pictures relate to each other. How are the two pictures you've selected similar? How are they different? Please talk about that in your small groups.** If students get stuck, encourage them to raise their hands so you or another adult can come and prod their thinking.

Ask students to return to one large group and invite anyone who wants to share about the relationship between the two pictures to do so. After a number of people have shared, ask:

Q: **What themes stood out in either your small-group or our large-group discussions?**

Q: **What feelings emerged in you during this process?**

Q: **What does this say about us as a group?**

Q: **What does this say about our time serving, and how that justice work relates to our lives now?**

Q: **How can what we've seen and discussed today help us go deeper in our justice work?**

Close in prayer, but ask your students to keep their eyes open as you pray, looking at the two pictures they've chosen. If it feels appropriate, invite some of your students to also pray aloud. Encourage students to take both pictures home and place them in a visible location as a reminder of how their justice work relates to home, and vice versa.

COST

BY RANA CHOI PARK

SOME
SCRIPTURE

BIG IDEA: Kingdom work is costly—but it's not just a matter of dollars and cents.

You'll need:

- Copies of **My Mission Experience** and **Mission Dollars** handouts (pages 177 and 178-179), and/or copies of the *Deep Justice Journeys Student Journal* (pages 134-139)

- Pens

- Markers

- Poster paper

- (HAVE MORE TIME? option: Copies of your church's missions budget)

- Ahead of time, complete the **My Mission Experience** and **Mission Dollars** handouts on your own, but leave the "You" section of the **Mission Dollars** handout blank. Consider giving students copies of the **Mission Dollars** handout you completed so they can easily fill in the numbers for the "Team," "Host Community," and "Our Church" sections. But students should fill in the "You" section themselves.

After your students arrive, lead the following discussion:

Q: **How much money do you think our recent justice work cost?**

Q: **What are some things our service experience cost us besides money?**

Q: **How do we know if the benefits of our work were worth the cost? What are some ways we could evaluate that cost?**

Distribute pens and the **My Mission Experience** handout to your students and explain: **Today we're going to look more closely at the cost of our service, and see how it matches up against all that we—and the locals who hosted us—gained.** Give students several minutes to complete their handouts and invite some students to share any answers they wrote down that seemed especially meaningful.

Next distribute the **Mission Dollars** handout to students, possibly along with a copy of your own previously completed **Mission Dollars** handout so students have at least somewhat educated guesses as to the cost to the team, the host community, and your church.

When students are finished, ask: **Which costs and/or benefits are especially significant to you? Why are they so significant to you?**

Q: **This handout focuses on direct time and money, but what are some other costs of our justice work for you personally? If students get stuck, give them ideas such as taking time off work, time away from friends, they didn't have as much energy to give to other tasks, they got tired, it was emotionally draining, etc.**

Q: **What are some costs for our team?**

Q: **What are some costs for our host community?**

Q: **What about for our church? What are some costs for our church?**

Invite students to turn to Luke 14:25-30. After you've read the passage, explain: **While Jesus was discussing the cost of following him in general, we can assume Jesus wants us to think through the cost of following him in various facets of discipleship, including our justice work.**

Q: **What are the implications of Jesus' words for the next time we do justice work?**

Explain: **One way to think about costs and benefits over the long term is to compare the costs of our justice journey with the money required to support a full-time missionary, which is somewhere in the neighborhood of $43,800/year, or $120/day. The cost of supporting a missionary family for a year is $83,950/year, or $230/day.**[25] **As we've seen, the actual cost of supporting a missionary is more than just the cash. What can our youth ministry do to support missionaries year-round? Using the categories of costs (money and others) we've discussed, what could we contribute to help share the cost of a full-time missionary?** Write their ideas on poster paper.

Q: **In addition to supporting a missionary, another way to think about costs and benefits is to consider giving our energy and funds directly to the host community and its leaders. What could we do that would support the host community that way? What would be some of the benefits of doing so?**

After you have listed students' ideas, explain: **We're going to get to vote on these ideas now. I'm going to give you each the power to write five dots next to the ideas on the poster paper. If you're a big fan of just one of the ideas, you can write five dots next to that one idea. If you're torn among five different ideas, you can write one dot next to five ideas. In other words, you can divide the dots any way you choose among any number of ideas (e.g., one idea gets two dots; a second idea gets three dots) but you can only make five dots total.** Give students pens so they can mark their five dots on their favorite ideas.

After students have finished, point out the two to five ideas that received the most dots. Ask: **How can we make these ideas a reality? Which of you would like to work with me and others on our adult team so we can bear the cost to help missionaries or give money directly to local leaders and ministries year-round?** If possible, write down students' names and form teams who can meet again in a few weeks so your ministry can get some traction in bearing the cost of justice work year-round.

HAVE MORE TIME?

Find out how your church is supporting missionaries, justice work, and economic development efforts around the world and share that information with your students. If possible, share an annual church missions report and get students' responses.

---

25. Estimates based on the Evangelical Lutheran Church in America Legacies newsletter, November 2006. See www.elca.org.

MY MISSION EXPERIENCE

Think back on our recent experience and answer the reflection questions below with words, phrases, or sentences:

Host Community

We were able to...

I think this made a difference because...

Me

I now see the world in a new way because...

I sensed God speaking to me or teaching me...

Our Team

Our team really grew in so many ways, such as...

Our Church

I think our justice work might inspire our church because...

MISSION DOLLARS

▶ PAGE 1 ◀

Complete the fields below based on our recent experience. It's okay to use your best estimates on time and money.

YOU

Funds you personally contributed or raised $_____

Time you contributed

        Preparation time: hours   _____

        Time serving: hours   _____

        Debrief time: hours   _____

        TOTAL HOURS   _____

Since your time is worth $____/hour, that's a total of $_____

TOTAL PERSONAL CONTRIBUTION $_____

TEAM

        Number of team members   _____

**MULTIPLY THE TOTAL YOU CONTRIBUTED BY
THE NUMBER OF TEAM MEMBERS. TOTAL TEAM CONTRIBUTION** $_____

HOST COMMUNITY

Funds contributed or raised $_____

My best guess on the number of hours the host community contributed to our work   _____

Since their time is worth $___/hour, that's a total of $_____

TOTAL HOST CONTRIBUTION $_____

OUR CHURCH

Funds contributed or raised $_____

My best guess on the number of hours members of my church contributed to our work
(through prayer, fundraisers, encouragement, providing transportation, etc.) ___

Since their time is worth $_____/hour, that's a total of $_____

TOTAL CHURCH CONTRIBUTION $_____

WHEN I ADD UP ALL FOUR BOXES, THE GRAND TOTAL IS $_____

I HAVE A DREAM

BY KARA POWELL

SOME SCRIPTURE

BIG IDEA: God's dreams for justice and the dignity of all persons become realities through people like us.

You'll need:

- The "I Have a Dream" PowerPoint available at www.fulleryouthinstitute.org

- Ahead of time, watch the timed PowerPoint sequence and decide if you'd like to add background music or play it in silence.

- Bibles

Welcome students and then ask: **What do you know about Dr. Martin Luther King Jr.?**

Explain that "I Have a Dream" was probably King's most famous speech. King spoke these words on August 28, 1963, during a march of 200,000 people in Washington, DC. At this point, play the "I Have a Dream" PowerPoint presentation.

Q: **How would you summarize Martin Luther King Jr.'s dream? As you think about that dream, how do you feel?**

Q: **How does Martin Luther King's dream mesh with our experience doing justice work?**

Q: **How does it mesh with what our life is like now that we're home?**

Q: **The last slide asks, "Today, what kingdom dreams are being birthed in you?" How would you answer that question?**

Q: **How, if at all, is your answer to that question different now from before our justice work?**

Q: **What advice would you give to someone who doesn't have any kingdom dreams at the moment?**

Q: **What motivates you to want to see your dreams become a reality?**

Q: **Based on what you experienced as you served, what part do you think you play in making those dreams become a reality? What part does God play?**

Adapted from Module 1 of FYI's "Your Kingdom Come," a curriculum done in partnership with World Vision's One Life program and available for free at www.fulleryouthinstitute.org.

At this point, distribute Bibles and explain you'd like to share a few verses that precede Amos 5:24, the verse in the PowerPoint. Read Amos 5:21-24 and ask:

Q: **Why do you think God refuses to accept the people's offerings and religious acts?**

Q: **What do you think it looks like to "let justice roll on like a river, righteousness like a never-failing stream"?**

Explain: **Amos 5:21-24 seems to indicate that our worship and our acts of justice are related—that raising our hands in worship is linked to opening our hands toward those who have been victims of oppression or injustice. As we move into a time of prayer and worship together, let's invite God to reveal the true condition of our worship to us, and to move us toward worship that flows out of deeply caring for God's world.**

Ask your students to gather into pairs or small groups and pray for one another's kingdom dreams. You might want to reread Amos 5:24 as a catalyst for prayer, asking God to bring justice that rolls like a river and righteousness like a never-failing stream. Invite students to ask God to provide the grace and strength they need to take steps forward—whether baby steps or large leaps—in seeing kingdom dreams become a reality. Close as appropriate to your setting with some sort of corporate worship, perhaps involving a time in which students can write their reflections on the connection between our worship and our actions toward those in need. Given the content of the passage, you may want to plan worship *without* music.[26]

---

26. For more thoughts on connecting worship and justice, see the FYI article "Just Worship" at www.fulleryouthinstitute.org.

NET WORTH

BY KARA POWELL

SOME SCRIPTURE

BIG IDEA: Serving in the kingdom of God reorients our ideas of personal value and net worth.

You'll need:

- Paper
- Pencils or pens
- Calculators
- A prize, if you choose to award one
- (HAVE MORE TIME? option: Copies of your church's annual budget)

This exercise involves students assessing the monetary worth of what they are wearing. Since you are the best gauge of your group, feel free to adapt this activity to fit your students' level of trust and vulnerability. Be especially aware of how differing income levels among the families of your students might make the exercise difficult for students whose "net worth" is lower than others in the group.

Welcome students and ask them to think back to your time serving together: **How did the locals we served use their money? How is that similar to how you and your family use it? How is it different?**

Give each student a piece of paper and pencil, and distribute as many calculators as possible to students. Explain: **Today each of us is going to total up his or her monetary value. I'd like you to calculate, to the best of your ability, how much money is represented at this moment on your person. In other words, what is your "net worth" right now? Make a guess at how much was spent (by you or someone else) on your shoes, jeans, jacket, purse, sunglasses, cell phone, jewelry, whatever is in your backpack or wallet, even your braces, the highlights in your hair...*anything* you can put a monetary value on. List all this stuff, and add up the total dollar amount. Do not share your estimate of your "net worth" with anyone else.**

Give students a few minutes to calculate their own total net worth. If you've not done so ahead of time, you should likewise calculate your own net worth.

Adapted from Vision Generation #4, a resource developed for World Vision and available at www.fulleryouthinstitute.org. Original idea from Mark Maines.

Lead the following discussion:

Q: **What was the experience of calculating your own net worth like for you?**

Q: **What made it easy to calculate your own net worth? What made it challenging?**

Q: **What, if anything, about this exercise surprised or shocked you? Describe your response to that surprise—does it make you want to do anything or does it raise any questions for you?**

At this point you might want to expand the conversation by highlighting an item most students have in common, like blue jeans or shoes, and pursue questions like:

Q: **How much money would you say is appropriate to spend on a pair of jeans? Should that amount be any different for someone who follows Christ? Why or why not?**

Q: **How do you think the locals we served on our justice mission would answer the question about how much is appropriate to spend on a pair of jeans?**

Q: **How, if at all, is your own willingness to spend money on yourself different from what you would have said before our justice work? Why do you think that is?** It's quite likely some students will say that their views about money were not significantly impacted by the time serving. If this is the case, consider carefully and lovingly exploring why that might be. The main point is to help connect the dots between the justice issues they encountered on their trip and justice in everyday life.

> Note what the rich ruler asks Jesus: "Good teacher, what must I *do* to inherit eternal life?" Ironically, Jesus had just taught in Mark 10:15 that the kingdom is more about *receiving* than *doing*.

Q: **Whether it's jeans, shoes, or the number of albums you download from iTunes, how do you determine when you have crossed a line into what is "excessive"? As people who want to serve others, when—if ever—is it okay to spend extravagantly on ourselves?**

Q: **When we cross the line into what is "excessive," what is the impact on us? How about on others?**

Q: **Here's a startling reality: U.S. citizens make up only 5 percent of the world's population, but we consume half the world's resources.[27] Given what we've seen in the midst of our service experience, how does that make you feel?** You may want to repeat this statistic to be sure students caught it.

At this point, ask a few students to read aloud the story of Jesus' encounter with the rich young ruler found in Mark 10:17-27.

Q: **This young man clearly had tried to honor God in many ways, but Jesus said one thing was missing. How would you describe in your own words what the man was missing?**

Q: **If Jesus told you to do the same thing he told this young man to do, how do you think you would respond?**

27. *The World Factbook* (2005 version): https://www.cia.gov/library/publications/the-world-factbook/index.html); International Database for the U.S. Census Bureau: http://www.census.gov/ipc/www/idb/.

Q: **In Mark 10:24, the disciples are "amazed" at Jesus' words. Perhaps that was because, like many religious people both past and present, they'd been told wealth was evidence a person was blessed by God. How is Jesus' teaching different from that common belief?**

Q: **So does Jesus intend for all his followers—including us—to sell all we have and give it to the poor? Why or why not?** Share that it may not have been this man's wealth itself that excluded him from following Jesus, but rather his inability to be generous with it or free to live without it. Jesus repeats several times that it is hard—particularly for the rich, but for everyone, really—to enter the kingdom of God. For some people, following Jesus may, in fact, require giving away everything they have. For everyone, it requires a new way of viewing possessions and personal worth.

Q: **How can we use what we've been given—our own net worth—in a spirit of extravagant generosity that offers deep justice and the gospel to others?**

Close your time with a journaling exercise, asking students to reflect on what they value and why. On the same paper they used to calculate their net worth, have them create a "Lowering my net worth" list—brainstorming ways they can reduce the costly material stuff that clutters their lives and then possibly redistribute some of that money and stuff to others. Feel free to invite students to work in pairs or even in small groups. Make sure to give a few final minutes for students to prayerfully ask the Lord to show them which of the "Lowering my net worth" ideas he might want them to implement.

HAVE MORE TIME?

Invite students to design their "ideal church budget." That is, if it were up to them, how and where would they spend the church's money? Instead of dealing with specific numbers, you might want to help students come up with the percentage of the budget they'd like to spend on each category.

When students are finished, distribute copies of your church's annual budget, explain where the money goes, and discuss the similarities or contrasts between their "ideal" budget and your church's budget. (You may also want to give some framework for how the church budget is determined in your church.) What part, if any, does caring for those in poverty have in your budget? What would your church need to do in order to have a greater impact beyond its own walls? Consider inviting someone from your church's finance committee to be part of this conversation.

A DOLLAR A DAY

BY KARA POWELL

BIG IDEA: More than one billion people around the world are forced to try to live on one dollar a day, but it's barely possible. We have the ability to make a difference in their lives, and we can start by praying on their behalf.

NO SCRIPTURE

You'll need:

- Enough dollar bills for (a) everyone in your group, (b) just a few, or (c) just you, depending on how you decide to carry this out

- (HAVE MORE TIME option: Magazine pictures, pictures of various parents and children, a picture of your youth group, paper, pens, markers or crayons, a mirror, a jar)

Welcome students and distribute a dollar bill to everyone in your group. If your budget doesn't allow for that, you could (a) ask everyone present who has a dollar with them to get it out, (b) bring up a few volunteers, give each of them a dollar, and then have them stand in front of the group holding their bills, or (c) hold up one dollar yourself, which you will later pass around. Then lead the following discussion:

> We *highly* recommend you incorporate the prayer labyrinth described in the HAVE MORE TIME? option for this exercise, so please try to schedule this activity when you have enough time for it.

Q: **With the dollar in your hand, what could you buy? What will a dollar purchase?**

Q: **If you could spend this dollar any way you chose, what would you most likely do with it?**

Q: **Most of you probably weren't thinking of answers like, "Pay the rent," "Buy food for my family," or "Get my little brother's prescription filled," right? Why is that?**

Q: **Do you think it's possible to live on one dollar a day? What if you had to do it? Describe how you might look at that dollar differently.**

Adapted from Vision Generation #3, a resource developed for World Vision and available at www.fulleryouthinstitute.org.

Continue: **The truth is, people can barely live on one dollar a day. There is no economy in the world where all basic needs can be met for the equivalent of one dollar a day. Yet, more than one BILLION people try to make it work. What's more, more than HALF THE WORLD'S POPULATION—THREE BILLION PEOPLE—live on just two dollars a day or less.**

Q: **As you think about the poverty we observed or experienced during our justice work, what do you think the people in that community have in common with those who live on one or two dollars per day? How do they differ?**

Continue: **In sub-Saharan Africa (where the impact of the deadly AIDS disease is currently hitting hardest), 45 percent of the people live on less than one dollar a day.**[28] **To be more specific, between 1990 and 2001, the average income in that region was around 60 cents a day.**

Q: **How many of you spent at least 60 cents to purchase something today? Raise your hands.**

Q: **As you hear these statistics, what emotions do you feel? What is your honest response?** Do your best to help them with this question. Check students' postures and body language for cues, and perhaps push them a bit to share their responses.

Explain: **Whether we spent 60 cents or 60 dollars on ourselves today, how can we discern the ways God wants us to use whatever we have—meaning all that God has given us—for the greatest possible good?**

One way to know how we can best use our money to help others is to pray. Today we're going to join with and pray for our brothers and sisters around the world who are forced to try to survive on less than a dollar a day.

As we pray, let's think about these dollar bills and start by repenting of our flippant use of money, our overspending on ourselves, or other ways we have not used our money wisely. I'm going to pass around this dollar and, if you want to, go ahead and pray your repentance prayer out loud when the dollar passes through your hands.

After you feel the time of repentance is over, transition to a different prayer emphasis: **Now I'd like us to pray that the Lord will take the resources we as well as those who are poor have and multiply them. I'm hoping several of you pray specifically for the locals we have recently served.** Let the prayer time last as long as feels appropriate, and consider closing with one or two worship songs.

---

28. To download and use a free youth ministry curriculum written by FYI to help you and your students discuss and respond to the worldwide AIDS pandemic, visit www.fulleryouthinstitute.org.

HAVE MORE TIME?

Convert a hallway near your youth room into a prayer labyrinth.[29] You might use the prayer station ideas below along the way, or create some of your own. Make sure you have paper, pens, and markers or crayons for Stations 2 and 3.

At the start of your labyrinth time, explain each station and invite students to proceed through the prayer stations at their own pace. Depending on the size of your group, consider asking different students to start at different stations to avoid any bottlenecks. Make sure students remain silent as they pray through the stations:

- **STATION 1: CONFESSION.** (Post a few advertisements for things we don't need from both guys' and girls' magazines.) Confess our flippant use of money, our overspending, or other ways our use of money has not honored God.

- **STATION 2: PARENTS.** (Post pictures of dads and moms from developing nations, or pictures of parents you met in your own recent justice work.) Dads and moms (or often grandparents, aunts, or uncles who take on the role of parents) carry most of the burden of feeding and caring for their families' needs. In countries where an individual makes less than one dollar a day, imagine how that causes parents to feel. Pray for parents who can't afford to care for their families. Write down words that describe how you would feel if you were responsible for taking care of someone and knew you could not. Give those words to Jesus.

- **STATION 3: CHILDREN.** (Post pictures of children of various ethnicities, engaged in different activities; if possible, include pictures of kids your youth ministry recently served.) Pray for children whose parents are dying of disease, whose parents can't afford to care for or feed them, who are unable to go to school, who are forced to work or beg, or who are sold. Write out prayers for those children using crayons, pens, and paper. (If your youth ministry sponsors a child through an organization like World Vision or Compassion International, have that child's picture present and give students an opportunity to write a prayer for that specific child.)

- **STATION 4: GOVERNMENTS.** (Post pictures of leaders of various governments including your own local, state, and national leaders.) Pray for wisdom for those who govern. Pray that their eyes would be opened to the needs around the world and that they would have wise responses to poverty. Pray for nations to help other nations.

- **STATION 5: ME, US.** (Have a mirror at this station and a picture of your youth group.) Pray that God will open your eyes to the needs around you. Pray for your youth ministry, that together you will be able to impact your community, nation, and world, and that the resources you give will be multiplied. Have a jar there for students to place their dollar bills in.

At the end of their time in the prayer labyrinth, bring the jar of bills in front of the whole group. Note that while a single dollar bill looks insignificant, when you put a bunch of bills together, you can begin to offer creative justice. Hand out the dollars to the students again, this time with the invitation to go and find a way to multiply this dollar. Ask students: **How could you invest this dollar—as well as other money you have—to make a difference in the lives of the poor, whether it be the poor you recently served or others around the world? What you do with this dollar is ultimately up to you, but imagine the justice possibilities...and pray about expanding this dollar.**

---

29. This prayer labyrinth was conceptualized by Cari Jenkins.

BAG IT

BY KARA POWELL

LOTSA SCRIPTURE

BIG IDEA: God wants us to make wise, ethical decisions with our money, which often means making sacrifices.

You'll need:

*   Shopping bags from places where your students spend money (fast-food places, sit-down restaurants, coffeehouses, movie theatres, clothing stores, electronics stores, etc.). Ideally, you'd get a bag from the actual store, but you could also label paper grocery bags for a low-tech, timesaving alternative.

*   One lunch-sized brown paper bag per student

*   Ten green slips of paper (cut to the approximate size of a dollar bill) for each student

*   Pens or pencils

*   Bibles

Q: **Where do you tend to spend your money? What are some of your favorite stores?**

Continue: **I'm going to place these bags at the front of the room. They represent the stores you've mentioned.** Feel free to add bags based on your students' answers. Every once in a while our kids surprise us with what they're doing!

I'm going to give 10 pieces of green paper to each of you. Imagine each slip is a $10 bill—so you all have $100. I want you to show us your spending habits in an average week by placing one or more $10 bills in the bags where you tend to spend your money. So, for example, if you spend an average of $30 a week at fast-food restaurants, put three of your $10 bills in that bag. Some students probably spend more than $100 a week, and some may spend a lot less. Try to help them think about their own spending as if they had $100 and not the usual amount of money they'd spend.

After students have finished placing their slips in the bags, ask for volunteers (students or adults) to take the bags somewhere out of sight and count the green pieces of paper in each bag. As the money is being counted, lead the following discussion with your students:

Adapted from Module 3 of FYI's "Your Kingdom Come", a curriculum done in partnership with World Vision's One Life program and available for free at www.fulleryouthinstitute.org.

Q: **Which bags do you think will have the most money in them? Which will have the least? How do you feel about that?**

Q: **How, if at all, are your spending habits different now from before we served? How does that feel?**

Q: **Do you think students who get their money by working treat their money differently than those who receive money from their parents? If so, how?**

When the money is counted, announce the final results. Compare students' predictions—about which bags would have the most and least money—with the actual results.

Q: **As we think about the people we recently served, what bags would they put their money in? How is that similar to the choices we'd make? How is it different?**

Q: **Do you think it's true that the way we spend our money reflects our priorities? Why or why not?**

Ask for a student volunteer to read aloud Matthew 6:19-24, an excerpt from the Sermon on the Mount.

Q: **In Jesus' day, moths and rust would destroy your stuff, and thieves could easily break through the mud bricks that comprised most of the houses in Palestine. There probably aren't too many of us here today who have lost our stuff to moths, rust, or thieves. If you were rewriting verse 19 in today's language, what would you say?**

Q: **What do you think Jesus means by "treasures in heaven"? How do we store those up for ourselves?**

Q: **Let's reread Matthew 6:21, since many theologians and Bible scholars think it's the key to the passage. What do we know about the role of the human heart in our bodies? What does that tell us about the role of our treasures in our lives?**

> When Jesus refers to a person's "heart," he doesn't mean the coronary organ inside our bodies. Instead, he means the center of our personalities, which embraces our minds, emotions, and wills.

Q: **Verses 22 and 23 are pretty strange, but think about where they're placed—right after verse 21 and right before verse 24. Given that the references to the "eye" are sandwiched between verses about money, what do you think Jesus is trying to say in verses 22 and 23?**

Q: **How might money become our master? If money is our master, how would that affect the way we participate in God's kingdom work?**

Q: **Now let's think about our shopping bags from earlier in the lesson. What have we learned about our own treasures from the ways we spend our money? How does that make you feel?**

Q: **I want you to think about this question but not answer it aloud. If we'd placed a bag labeled "Giving to Others" among the other bags, how much of your money would have gone in that bag?** Feel free to make the "Others" more specific by referring to the people your ministry recently served. **How does your honest response to that question make you feel?**

At this point, distribute one lunch-sized brown paper bag and a pen to each of your students. Give your students a few minutes to prayerfully reflect on how they spend their money, and how their recent justice work, as well as this discussion, might be nudging them toward different decisions. Invite them to write any changes they'd like to make with their money on the outside of their brown paper bag. When they are finished, you can either collect them and read students' decisions aloud (though you may want to do this anonymously), or you can ask your students to hang on to them and keep them in a visible location in their homes or cars as an ongoing reminder of the deeper commitments they are making with their money.

REWIND AND FAST FORWARD

BY KARA POWELL

BIG IDEA: A few weeks after our justice work, it's a good idea to rewind time to remind ourselves of how we were impacted, and then fast forward to think about how we can better support one another in the future.

You'll need:

- Ahead of time, record some of your team's final debrief discussion(s) on audio or video. If you have time and/or a student who's into media stuff, you might want to edit out some of the inevitable peripheral chatter. If you don't have time or a techie-student, then make sure you have ample time to play the recording and then lead the discussion.

- A way to play that audio or video

- Whiteboard or poster paper

- Water bottles

- Rocks

- A large bowl

- Pens

Greet students and point out how long it's been since your justice mission. Distribute a rock and a water bottle to each student as you explain: **I've learned that God's change process often resembles the way water shapes rock. Let's think for a moment about all the different ways water shapes rock:**

- **God's transformation can seem slow at times, as if we're a stone in a creek being smoothed.**

- **Sometimes it can even seem too slow, as if we're just a stone sitting in the middle of a pond and nothing much is happening.**

- **Or sometimes it seems quick, like a rushing river flowing over stones in its path.**

- **Other times it seems overwhelming, making us seem vulnerable, like a rock being pelted under a huge waterfall.**

Q: **In what other ways is God's transformation similar to the ways water shapes rock?**

Q: **Of all these water/rock images we've been discussing, which seems to resonate most with the way God's been changing you during and/or since our justice work?**

After a few students have shared, continue: **In the midst of God's work in our lives, I know it's sometimes hard to remember all we experienced and reflected on together, so today we're going to do a bit of rewinding. Literally. We're going to watch (or listen) to our debrief discussion, but as we're watching, I want us to stay alert for ways we were impacted—either as individuals or as a group.**

If you hear something that reflects a way our justice work affected us, I want you to come up and write it on the whiteboard even as the video continues to play. You can write emotions, attitudes, ways of thinking, behaviors/actions, or any other area of impact you think of as you re-experience our debrief conversation.

After the video has ended, lead the following discussion:

Q: **What themes do you see in the ways we were impacted?**

Q: **How have these themes, or any of these individual ideas, made a difference in your life since our justice work?**

Q: **Let's be honest: What decisions or commitments did you make during or immediately after our service that haven't gone so well? Why do you think that is?**

Q: **Are there decisions or commitments you'd like to revise based either on the video we just saw or on what life is like now that you're back home?**

Q: **Let's fast forward and think about the next month. What can we do to support one another in living up to these commitments for the next month?**

Divide up into pairs or small groups, and ask students to exchange rocks so they are now holding their partner's rock. Give students plenty of time to pray that the Lord will empower them by his grace and continue to transform them into the people he wants them to be now that they are back home. Consider inviting your students to keep their prayer partner's rock as a reminder to pray for God's ongoing work in their partner's life.